"I think about multiethnicity a lot, I have beloved family members who are multiethnic, and I pastor a diverse congregation. And yet, as Chandra's book makes plain, I still have so much to learn about the experiences—the pains and the joys—of those who don't neatly fit into monoethnic categories. With the sure footing of one who has lived the experience, Chandra invites those of us who haven't to listen carefully and to imagine ways of following Jesus together that are hospitable to everyone. *Mixed Blessing* is required reading for anyone who wants a glimpse of the complex and hopeful future of the church in this country."

David W. Swanson, pastor and author of *Rediscipling the White Church*

"There is such a huge need for this book! I have often wondered who in the next generation would write about the mixed-race experience from a Christian perspective, and I am so glad it is Chandra Crane. At once reassuring and challenging, Chandra invites multiethnic people both to rest in the knowledge of being 'loved and lovely,' and to rise up and take our rightful place in the Beloved Community, using our pain and privilege to do the work of creating welcoming spaces for all. I highly recommend this book to anyone wanting to help heal our multiethnic selves and world."

Sundee T. Frazier, author of *Check All That Apply: Finding Wholeness as a Multiracial Person* and several novels for young people featuring interracial families and mixed-race people

"We live in a society that values placing people into neat categories and tidy boxes. Chandra Crane's important book *Mixed Blessing* speaks a needed word about the complexities and blessings of embodying a multiethnic identity in a world that often overlooks these voices. As a White person, this book has opened my eyes and helped me begin to better understand the experience of multiethnic people, something that will help me better minister in my church and in my community."

April Fiet, pastor of First Presbyterian Church in Scottsbluff, Nebraska

"This book should become an instant classic—a moving, wise, knowing guide for those of biracial or multiethnic backgrounds who so often feel *other*. Chandra Crane gets it! But it is also necessary reading for all who need to hear more intimately the stories of our friends, coworkers, and neighbors, and thereby understand the sometimes perplexing new vocabularies we need if we are to honor the hopes and dreams of all of God's image bearers. Chandra Crane is painfully honest—her writing made us cry—yet *Mixed Blessing* is upbeat and interesting and full of gospel hope. We need this book now more than ever."

Beth and Byron Borger, Hearts & Minds Bookstore in Dallastown, Pennsylvania

"As Chandra Crane says, 'Don't be colorblind. Be color brave.' I agree!"

Doug Schaupp, national director of evangelism for InterVarsity Christian Fellowship/USA and coauthor of *Breaking the Huddle*

"This is the book I've been waiting for! As a person of mixed ethnicity, I've long struggled to know who I am, where I belong, and how to faithfully embrace and engage both the privilege and burden of straddling multiple worlds. Chandra is a wise and compassionate guide for all of us who walk these winding paths or seek to love and serve those who do."

Ben Lowe, cochair of Christians for Social Action and author of *Doing Good Without Giving Up*

"Building on her story as a Christian of mixed ethnicity, Chandra writes a deeply challenging book. There is no self-pity, even as she dissects what it is to be treated as *other*. Rather, the joy in her biblical studies is infectious as she writes of learning to image Jesus in all the complexity of personhood, and of the special place multiethnic believers can have in the modern church, showcasing God's present and future community. I warmly commend this gospel-focused book that will encourage those identifying as mixed race and inspire others (like me) to listen and learn afresh."

Paul Gardner, lecturer in biblical studies and author of the *Zondervan Encyclopedia of Bible Characters*

"My wife and I have had many conversations about the reality and difficulty of raising multiethnic and multicultural sons in today's racialized society. Thankfully, Chandra Crane's *Mixed Blessing* has stepped into the gap and helped us navigate these oftentimes unclear waters. This book is an essential read for all multiethnic and multicultural families and one my wife and I will constantly dive into as we raise our mixed blessings and show them the gift of their mixed identities."

Lamont English, assistant director, West Coast hub of Mission to the World (PCA)

"Integrating biblical narratives, personal story, and a variety of individuals' experiences, Chandra addresses the complexity of multiracial identity with nuance and insight. This book is everything I needed for the 'mixed' students, neighbors, and family members in my life. Most importantly, I found a framework I need to parent my own biracial sons."

Sandra Maria Van Opstal, executive director of Chasing Justice and author of *The Next Worship*

"I have told so many different people that this book is coming, and I'm so glad it's here. In an increasingly multiethnic, multiracial, and multicultural world, we need spiritual guides to help us navigate that growing complexity and diversity. This book serves as a helpful roadmap for all who don't fall neatly along preconceived ethnic, cultural, and racial lines—and who want to live as kingdom witnesses in the beauty of their complexity and heritage."

Sarah Shin, speaker and author of *Beyond Colorblind*

"The United States is in the early stages of a profound racial and ethnic 'mestizaje,' in which cultural groups from every continent on the globe are freely mixing in a historically unprecedented way. Chandra Crane shows us that this is by God's design and offers an honest and hopeful roadmap for navigating these new cultural realities."

Robert Chao Romero, author of *Brown Church: Five Centuries of Latina/o Social Justice, Theology, and Identity*

"Chandra Crane takes a wonderfully multivalent approach at examining multiethnicity, exploring nuances (both seen as well as unseen) and their no-less-real ramifications. This book serves well—not only for multiethnic people to understand themselves better but also for those who do not inhabit such a world—to empower us all to love our neighbor better, for the good of God's kingdom. The author is direct with the lessons that would be helpful for the world to know, but at the same time she unpacks the beauty behind these sometimes-challenging complexities."

Allen Yeh, associate professor of intercultural studies and missiology at Biola University

"Those of us who are of mixed ethnicity defy categories, stump those trying to pin us down, and can even stump ourselves while trying to figure out our own identities. Where do we belong? Where do we fit in? Will we ever feel at home? It is clear that in *Mixed Blessing* Chandra Crane has done her homework and has done the interior work to detail for the rest of us the complexity, beauty, and gift of being a multiethnic person. She also shares some real but hard truths about how we are 'othered' by others. In reading *Mixed Blessing*, I felt seen and understood. This a welcomed and needed resource!"

Marlena Graves, author of *The Way Up Is Down: Becoming Yourself by Forgetting Yourself*

Mixed Blessing

CHANDRA
CRANE

Embracing the Fullness of Your Multiethnic Identity

FOREWORD BY
JEMAR TISBY

An imprint of InterVarsity Press
Downers Grove, Illinois

InterVarsity Press
P.O. Box 1400, Downers Grove, IL 60515-1426
ivpress.com
email@ivpress.com

InterVarsity Press® is the book-publishing division of InterVarsity Christian Fellowship/USA®, a movement of students and faculty active on campus at hundreds of universities, colleges, and schools of nursing in the United States of America, and a member movement of the International Fellowship of Evangelical Students. For information about local and regional activities, visit intervarsity.org.

While any stories in this book are true, some names and identifying information may have been changed to protect the privacy of individuals.

Cover design and image composite: David Fassett
Interior design: Daniel van Loon
Image: line drawing of woman's face: © ANASTASIIA DMITRIEVA / iStock / Getty Images Plus
Author photo by Acorn Studio. Hair and makeup by Gellisa A. Fevrier.

ISBN 978-0-8308-4805-8 (print)
ISBN 978-0-8308-4806-5 (digital)

Printed in the United States of America ♾

InterVarsity Press is committed to ecological stewardship and to the conservation of natural resources in all our operations. This book was printed using sustainably sourced paper.

Library of Congress Cataloging-in-Publication Data
A catalog record for this book is available from the Library of Congress.

P   25   24   23   22   21   20   19   18   17   16   15   14   13   12   11   10   9   8   7   6   5   4   3   2   1
Y   37   36   35   34   33   32   31   30   29   28   27   26   25   24   23   22   21   20

For Kennan, my favorite multicultural White guy.
My best friend, love, and ally—I couldn't have written this book without you.

For Annabel Sarai and Emmaline Janae,
*walking monuments of God's faithfulness
(and sense of humor).
Children of my heart and body—this book is for you.*

Contents

Foreword

Jemar Tisby

BACK WHEN I WAS A SCHOOLTEACHER, I had a coworker who always sorted her Skittles before she ate them. She would take the bag, dump out the candies on a clean surface, and then methodically group them into categories: orange with orange, red with red, and so on. She did it because she was hyper-organized and always had to have items neatly situated. She also did it because she wanted to enjoy each flavor one at a time without any mixing of colors. She wanted to "taste the rainbow"—but not all at once.

We often try to do with people what this teacher did with Skittles. Sort and place and categorize. When it comes to race and ethnicity, we want to drop people into carefully labeled slots: Black, White, Asian, Native, and more. But what happens when our convenient categories don't work (not that they ever did)? What happens to the people who have a blend of backgrounds? Where do we situate others and ourselves when the colors, cultures, languages, and aesthetics are mixed?

In her debut book, *Mixed Blessing*, Chandra Crane illuminates the underappreciated reality that people of mixed racial and ethnic background defy our simplistic social groupings. All of us have felt a sense of alienation and the awkwardness of not quite fitting in, but multiethnic people have an acute sense of this. Through her personal journey as well as a sensitive examination of other multiethnic stories, Chandra reveals the burden and privilege of living in the racial and ethnic "in-between" in one's embodied self.

If you, like me, think of yourself as reasonably informed about racial dynamics, prepare to be humbled. Chandra's deft descriptions of the particularities of the multiethnic experience reveal in new ways the absurdities of racial categorizations while also offering insights to which few monoculture or monoethnic people are privy. She shows the clunkiness of language (aren't we all "people of color"?) and the fluidity of racial and ethnic categories that often rely on specious assumptions about skin color, patterns of speech, or social networks. She does this all while centering her examination on the truth that we are all created in the image of God. *Mixed Blessing* reminds us that people are not created for boxes but for God's glory.

This book helps fill an inexcusable gap in our understandings of racial and ethnic dynamics. It goes beyond the simple vectors of "White" and "Black" to show the spectrum of biological and cultural stories that so many people inhabit. Most of all, Chandra's book helps multiethnic people feel seen. In the Gospels, Jesus' miracles of healing and mercy often follow a formula. Jesus sees, he has compassion, and he acts. *Mixed Blessing* allows people whose experiences do not fit into predetermined categories to be seen. It renders their reality visible to a broad audience. It is then up to the reader to desire racial and ethnic justice and to act compassionately to bring about a more inclusive future.

Is *Mixed Blessing* an easy read? Certainly not. But it is an essential one.

Introduction

What Are You?

"SO WHAT *ARE* YOU, EXACTLY?"

I'm asked that often. When people see my dark-black and curly hair, my somewhat "almond-shaped" eyes, my pale skin with a yellow undertone—*and yet freckles*—they wonder. They can't place my ethnicity in a box, so they feel unsettled, maybe even threatened.

Depending on my mood, I choose one of a few answers. If I'm feeling sarcastic: "I'm human, thanks. And you?" Or if I'm feeling cryptic: "*Exotic*, obviously." If I'm feeling sarcastic and preachy: "Me? I'm part of the Colossians 3:12 'Beloved Community,'[1] part of God's people that he loves from the center of his being."

I've also learned to play dumb, answering with my own question: "Oh, how do you mean? Are you asking about my Myers-Briggs personality profile or maybe my Enneagram?" Obviously, they aren't. But hoping they'll actually hear themselves, I like to make people say it: "No, what ethnicity are you? Where are you from? Why do you look so *different?*"

What ethnicity am I, indeed.

A HARD QUESTION

If I'm feeling patient, loving, and strong enough, I invite folks to hear my story. They'd better get comfortable, because it takes a while. When the Holy Spirit leads me in being gracious, I answer that awkward question by sharing about my Thai national birthfather and my European American mom. Then I share about my African American dad, who married my mom and adopted me when I was five. I talk about being a proud New Mexican—born and raised. I share about my first trip to Thailand, in my early thirties, to see my paternal birth family. I mention my multiethnic church family in Mississippi, the heart of the Deep South. I also share that being a campus minister has shaped my heart to see diverse groups of students and faculty come together and learn more about Jesus. I explain that being an author gives me the privilege of hearing and sharing others' stories, even as I keep figuring out my own life story.

Within these pages, you will indeed find more than just my story; you will find *our* story. I'm so grateful for those who've been willing to fill out surveys and do interviews about their own experiences of being multiethnic and multicultural. They've generously given permission for their stories to be included (some with a real name and others with a pseudonym), having shared their time and their very selves. The heart of our mixed story is that no one person can embody multiethnicity in its entirety; we need each other so we can place ourselves in God's larger narrative.

"What are you?" is so multilayered. Sometimes I do want to talk about my mixed heritage and family of origin. Sometimes I want to talk about my current family or my various work and creative projects. And sometimes I just want to talk about a book I'm reading, a dessert I enjoy, or whatever ridiculous TV show I'm watching. We all deserve to be seen as more than just our ethnic appearance, as much as it is an important part of our story.

WHAT DEFINES US?

Multiethnic folks experience a series of defining moments—some painfully formative, others more joyful. Essential in the development of my mixed ethnic identity was the first time I was asked, "What *are* you?" in early grade school—but also when, by middle school, the question was actually *painful* rather than just confusing. There's the moment in my early years when I realized just how different my family is from everybody else's—and then the moment, not long after, when I realized just how different I am, even from everyone *in my family*. There's the first time I read the landmark book *Check All That Apply*[2] and heard that my mixed ethnicity was intentional and good, not an accident. And there's my experience of joining a multiethnic church, and finally, after more than three decades, feeling like I was home. There's also the first time, at a very young age, in which I was asked if I was adopted and the first time someone assumed my childhood best friend was my mother's daughter—not me—because I looked nothing like my mom.

Mercifully there was a moment in high school when I realized that being unique can have its advantages, to go along with the alienation. But there was also the first time I remember actually despising my mixed heritage. And then there were the school discussions about genetics and ethnicity—and how I despised others for pointing out my differences. These seemingly singular moments can combine over the years to create an overwhelming narrative of loneliness and alienation, even when there's joy and security too.

Another recent defining moment was when I wrote a chapter for an anthology. It took me—no exaggeration—five footnotes to explain my ethnic and cultural background. Five. Readers will no doubt be tired after reading so many footnotes, so imagine how exhausted I was after writing them. It was the first time I'd seen the complication of my multiethnicity in print—in black and white, if you will. As a mixed person, I don't have the option of an easy answer—minus footnotes—to the perpetual question "What exactly *are* you?" Understanding my ethnicity takes time.

If people seem to be asking out of genuine curiosity, I share everything in those five footnotes. If folks are still with me, I share about the joy, and the pain, of being multiethnic and multi*cultural*. If they lose interest, I shrug, trying not to be wounded by it. I'm used to people being overwhelmed by me and my complexity. I'm used to people who want a simple, comfortable place to land. I know people can react badly when they doubt their own place in the world because I wreck their preconceived notions.

NOT FITTING IN

Because being multiethnic and multicultural can mean never really fitting in—with strangers, but perhaps even more so with family—I have an almost perpetual sense of displacement. I'm obviously White with my Black family, awkwardly American with my Thai family, and confusingly "ethnic" with my White family. My mixed story means my kids also are inescapably multiethnic. Even if I had managed to find a racially Thai/White *and* culturally Black/White husband (God did bless me with a White man who has a heart for racial reconciliation[3]), my multiethnicity means that my children, too, are pretty much guaranteed a "mixed marriage."

Being mixed can also mean never really being at home in one's own skin—a feeling of constant *otherness*. For a long time, it meant resenting my very self, because I stir up questions wherever I go. Even if I'm the only person in the room, the damning question reverberates in my head. I hear not just *What am I?* but also the heart of it, the frightening underlying message that *if no one can tell what I am, maybe I'm not much of anything*.

Perhaps you resonate with this. You picked up this book because you're mixed, and you're weary from feeling stuck in the middle or being forced to choose sides. Or maybe you're intrigued by your multiethnicity and wonder where to go next. Perhaps you're interested not because you're multiethnic, but your child, best friend, neighbor, or coworker is. You're hoping to find ways to better understand and love people, to celebrate them in their fullness. Or perhaps you're curious because you've noticed more and more people who defy description and don't fit into neat categories.

No matter why you're reading this, I welcome you with a special invitation: meet God here. Meet with the Lord Jesus, who knows what it's like to be multiethnic due to his Jewish, Canaanite, and Moabite heritage. Receive anew healing and a sense of calling from the precious King Jesus, who knows what it means to live in liminal spaces and on the margins. On earth, he was a minority; and in heaven, though he even now sits on the throne, he also waits for his kingdom to come fully and his will to be done perfectly.

Walk with the merciful God who also knows what it's like to be multicultural, because he's the ultimate multi*every-thing*, incomprehensibly the "one person, two natures," three-in-one, triune God. He is the θεανθρωπος (*thean-thropos*)—the God-man, the ultimate "both/and," whose incarnation and atoning sacrifice make racial reconciliation—reconciliation of any kind—actually possible between fallen people. Author Sundee Frazier reminds us that Jesus show-cased physical and spiritual reconciliation in his very being, and we mixed folks have the unique privilege of reflecting his image in our multiethnicity.[4]

Do you believe that being ethnically mixed is a privilege? If I'm honest, I have to ask: Do I? As with everything else tied up in multiethnicity, the answer is yes, no, and everything in-between. Some days—maybe even most days—I'm grateful for my ethnic story. Other days, it's hard to focus on the joy of multiethnicity instead of the grief. This is especially true when I'm asked "What *are* you?" several times, or when people assume I'm monoethnically White, missing the other parts of my story.

Being mixed means being a stranger and sojourner wherever one goes, in every sense of the phrase. But that's not always bad. Let's explore the *pain* and the *privilege* of the multiethnic reality, but also the *promise*—the redemptive impact mixed folks can have on the world and in the church. Let's find joy in how our lives echo the creation-fall-redemption narrative woven throughout the Bible. A real gospel hope is displayed in what God is doing through us.

Whether you were raised in the church—that is, you've never known a day you didn't believe in Jesus—or you accepted Christ in a dramatic conversion, you are welcome here. Whether you've walked this narrow, precious path for a lifetime or just a short time, this is your story too. And whether you've heard the name of Jesus before or this is your first time learning about this working-class multiethnic minority from backwater Galilee, come and see. See the face of him who—you will discover—doesn't look that different from you, no matter your skin tone. See the joy of him who rejoices when a lost sheep is found, when a lost child comes home.

Like Moses (who minister Neil Rendall tells us was multicultural, knew the tension of living in different worlds and had his own questions of identity),[5] we are strangers in a strange land in the here and now (Ex 2:22). Yet we who follow Christ do have a home. So, dear siblings, trusting in Jesus means citizenship in a kingdom that bases our ultimate value on belonging to Christ, not in our ethnic identity. And yet— *and yet*—this kingdom does not obliterate the beauty of our individual ethnic and cultural stories. The kingdom of God establishes our primary Christian identity *without us losing the value of our ethnic identity.*

Our identity as part of the redeemed family actually gives our ethnic identity the most joy and meaning—our place in the story. All believers are indeed on a journey, traveling together to, as author C. S. Lewis puts it, a "far-off country"[6] for which we long.

As we begin this specific leg of the journey—to a better understanding who we are as a mixed people—remember that you are not alone. Though it's not easy to live in community with other fallen humans, we are indeed traveling in the company of that Colossians 3:12 fellowship: God's chosen people, beloved and safe. So let's journey together, with Jesus, in this deep, satisfying day-to-day walk as precious, created people eagerly awaiting our completion.

CHAPTER ONE

Multiethnicity 101

The Foundation of Being Mixed

"WHY DOES SHE LOOK LIKE CHINA?" stage-whispered the little boy upon seeing my younger daughter. At the age of three, she was already being confronted with the stereotype that her eyes were more narrow than "normal" and the assumption she was therefore Chinese. The boy's dad was mortified and apologetic, but I wasn't surprised by the interaction. I was glad to share about her ethnicity—that she has White and Thai ancestry (not Chinese). But I think what truly confused the little boy was that our daughter looked *"like"* an Asian. He had no category for her mixed features: her light-brown hair and ruddy cheeks to go along with her oval eyes. She disrupted his expectations.

As my husband and I teach our kids about themselves, the world, and where they fit into the story, we want their mixed ethnicity to be a comfortable truth that they grow into, not something to spring on them "once they're older." That's a hard concept to explain, though: what being multiethnically Asian means, what features are considered Asian, why folks will probably assume she's Chinese. The story of being mixed is one of pain and privilege, created goodness and redeemed joy; but how do we define *mixed* as a concept? It's hard to boil down a complex idea to a concise definition, especially when the heart of the matter—being multiethnic—is that of being more than one thing.

Here's one simple definition: *being multiethnic is having two or more ethnic and/or racial backgrounds with significant differences.* But this leads us to ask, what is an ethnic or racial background? What, if anything, is the difference between ethnicity and race? Some may even ask, "Isn't race just made up? Aren't we all part of the human race?" These are important questions with complicated answers.

DEFINING TERMS, DEFINING REALITY

"Race" is indeed a social construct, as activist Ta-Nehisi Coates explains, not a biological reality.[1] While human DNA does vary, it's more by geography than by skin tone or other features, explains author Megan Gannon.[2] But the false biological nature of race makes it no less defining for us people of color. Race is a very real political and social reality. The modern idea of racial categories was created by those in power to keep their power (and, therefore, their wealth)—those who "chose dividends over dignity,"[3] as author and historian Jemar Tisby puts it. Though race is a fabrication, it is a powerful one.

The truth is, as Coates continues, that "*no coherent, fixed definition of race actually exists. . . .* The strongest argument for 'race' is that people who trace their ancestry back to Europe, and . . . sub-Saharan Africa, and . . . Asia, and . . . the early Americas, lived isolated from each other for long periods and have evolved different physical traits." The reasons that people with vastly different phenotypes—those distinct features usually associated with different ethnicities—can all check the same race box on the census goes "right back to the fact of race as a social construct. And an American-centered social construct."[4]

The United States census lists the five basic race categories as White, Black, Asian, American Indian, and Pacific Islander.[5] In contrast *Hispanic* is listed as an ethnic category. According to the US Census Bureau, "though many respondents expect to see a Hispanic, Latino, or Spanish category on the race question, this question is asked separately because people of Hispanic[6] origin may be of any race(s)."[7] While this appears to be an attempt to ensure that minority and vulnerable people are counted in the census, it adds a confusing distinction between race and ethnicity that isn't made in other forms and surveys.

From a general perspective, due to our nation's sociopolitical constructs, Americans understand there to be five racial categories: White, Black, Latinx, Asian, and Indigenous Peoples (or Native American). As globalization continues to increase, and as White people do the work of looking at their own ancestry, categories like Middle Eastern, South Asian, Jewish, Pacific Islander—and even European[8]— enter and reenter the American consciousness. The idea of race changes over time, but one constant is that it affects us all.

In popular culture, *race* and *ethnicity* often are used interchangeably to describe certain people groups who share characteristics in appearance (such as skin tone, facial features, body type, etc.). But even more confusingly, when average American citizens refer to someone of a certain race or ethnicity, they could actually be referring to a specific *culture* that has certain identifiers based on common cultural artifacts (as defined by author Andy Crouch),[9] behaviors, and standards. While being seen as "Black" in Western culture is predicated on one's skin tone, the descriptor is also tied to stereotypical cultural aspects, such as styles of dress, music, food, and self-expression (as well as the majority-culture judgments against them).

Conversely, being Asian is usually thought of less in terms of skin tone and more in terms of where one comes from (with the assumption being that it's not America), especially in the age of the coronavirus. Regardless, those of Asian descent are still judged by appearance—eye shape, hair texture, and other physical features—and more insidiously, by what that supposedly means about moral character.

THE HAVES, HAVE-NOTS, AND HAVE-A-LOTS?

The fact remains that however many races we may claim there are (or are not), many people think in terms of only two categories: White and nonwhite/colored.[10] There are "people," and then there are "people of color."[11] This is both true and untrue, both helpful and troublesome. We people of color have unique experiences that White folks do not have, but certain phrases can really limit communication, especially across different cultural groups. When everything is in contrast to and centered around the concept of "whiteness," it can be hard to erase the lines that have been drawn.

A similar either/or category, one that avoids some of these issues (while no doubt creating others), is that of the "haves" and the "have-nots." Power and privilege follow racial lines, so it's important to make this distinction, not to *create* categories but to acknowledge categories that already exist. Those categories were created and are reinforced by those who want to keep power and remain the "haves." On the other hand, the nature of the two categories points out and upholds the faulty logic of "White" in contrast to everything else. Black and Brown folks aren't simply White people who have been left in the oven too long. Lighter-skinned people of color aren't just White people with "exotic" garnishes. Whiteness (encompassing White culture and norms) is not the biblical standard from which everything else is derived, despite the prevailing majority-culture sentiment.

THE GIFT OF ETHNICITY TO THE NATIONS

This brings us to personal and biblical categories of ethnicity, culture, and race. We must ask this question: If we agree to see race as a social concept with real power behind it, what about ethnicity? When it's separated out from *race, ethnicity* is actually a biblical category. When looking at identity, the generally accepted cultural practice is to rank racial categories as primary, with ethnicity as a subset. But I like to follow the Bible's lead and flip the script. So I often use *ethnicity* (defined by national, cultural, and familial ties) as a main descriptor. When we focus on the diverse goodness of all humans as created in the image of God, and put emphasis on family affiliation and social interactions rather than race, then *race* can become an out-of-date footnote to the main text of our ethnicity. In thinking about her identity, Cheryl, who is both ethnically mixed and a transracial adoptee, thanks "God for his creativity in making people so unique and different . . . and what each person can bring to the world."

In seeing ethnicity as healthy and prescriptive—not merely descriptive—the Bible sets the precedent. As Efrem Smith writes, "Although race is not biblical, ethnicity is. We see groups of people described by ethnicity, nationality, and tribe within the scriptures. . . . When we look through scripture, we see the interplay of ethnicity and the way race came to be and see how Jesus is the fruit of a long and diverse bloodline."[12] Ethnicity is no accident. According to Sundee Frazier, "Part of God's plan for our world seems to include the creation of distinctive people groups, each with its own language, values, practices, even physical attributes. . . . God has planted within each ethnic group an element of his wisdom and character. . . . This makes each group crucial in God's plan to reveal his glory to the world."[13]

Shall we say that a little louder for the people in the back? Each and every ethnic group is part of how God reveals his glory. White supremacy can take a seat, thank you very much. The variety of ethnicities is not a curse that God needs to redeem. It is God's gift to the nations; he has revealed part of himself in the diversity of his image bearers, personified in the incarnation of Jesus.

Some folks look at ethnicity as being primarily a matter of skin tone, while others focus more on people groups. Some folks look further back, to the geography of ancestors and the significance of belonging to a place and family. Author Akemi Johnson defines *hapa* as "a transliteration of the English word 'half'" and the "Hawaiian word for 'part.'" Referring to an interview with Kealalokahi Losch, Johnson says, "Because the Hawaiian kingdom was more concerned with genealogy than race, . . . if you could trace your lineage to a Hawaiian ancestor, you were Hawaiian. Mixed Hawaiian did not mean less Hawaiian."[14] Indigenous Hawaiians tend to have strong ties to the land, and this has shaped their general acceptance of mixed folks.[15]

As someone with White, Chinese, and Pacific Islander roots, Morgan is able to embrace the term *hapa* as being part of her story growing up in California and visiting grandparents in Hawai'i. When sharing about the importance of place and how it shapes her identity, she reminds us that her "Hawaiian and Chinese ancestors' lives preceded the US annexation." Similar to Latinx/Mexican folks, "they didn't cross the border, the border crossed them."[16] Wherever we mixed folks locate our ethnicity, we can rest assured that it's ultimately from the Lord.

DIVERSITY AND DISTINCTIONS

Our multiethnicity deserves to be acknowledged and honored as we seek refuge, solace, healing, and growth. Even as we follow our ancestors in their unique ways of extending welcome, we need to draw boundaries. To use an analogy often employed when discussing race relations, our table of hospitality has seats for all, *but not for all to set the agenda.* Mixed folks, this is our space to celebrate, mourn, squabble (like any family does), rest, and break bread together. This is our multiethnic community.

This space we're entering is foremost for us multiethnic (and thus multicultural) folk who need and deserve a safe space to be the norm—not the exception—perhaps for the first time. So to have the right number of place settings at our table, there are two main distinctions to identify those of us who are mixed and whose stories are essential to this fellowship:

- One distinction is being *raised within a family consisting of two or more different and/or adversarial ethnic cultures* (especially as opposed to someone who comes into another ethnic culture as an adult). This unique upbringing can have both a richness of experience but also a sense of self-disconnect. These issues tend to play out more in terms of culture than of phenotypical appearance, though both are a factor.

- The other distinction is finding oneself, due to this diversity of family origins, *often in the ethnic minority within family and society*, whether in terms of appearance, learned cultural norms, or ethnically related issues of justice, etc. This experience can foster a sense of awareness and care for the *other* but also can lead to feeling like a perpetual *other*. These dynamics are often rooted in phenotype, but not to the exclusion of cultural norms.

Both categories can be fostered by a disconnect—even if only on the part of others—between the expectations of us and the reality. This can happen in multiple ways. Our physical appearance, communication styles, and experiences can leave us in the minority within many spheres of influence (whether that be family, school, church, work, or community). However, a strong sense of connection—with our own culture and with others' cultures—can also be created due to our shifting experiences. Just as there are many ways of embodying different family roles, ethnicities, genders, and sexualities, there is no *one* way to be multiethnic. How each of us chooses to tell our individual story depends on our temperament and situation. And while there are definitely healthy and unhealthy ways of being mixed, these are based on a universal human truth: how we relate to our mixed redeemer.

GROWING IN NUMBERS, CHANGING THE CULTURE

Although White normativity still has a stranglehold on the United States, we're living in a significant cultural shift where the group classified as "minorities" is fast becoming the majority percentage of the population, as research has revealed.[17] And even as mixed children are nothing new, with mixed marriages (finally) being declared legal for more than fifty years, demographics continue to change as generations of mixed folks are having children and even grandchildren who identify as multiethnic. Actor Zoë Kravitz is the daughter of Lisa Bonet and Lenny Kravitz, both of whom are half Black and half of Ashkenazi Jewish heritage, furthering the definition and experience of being mixed. My children have known about fractions from a young age, and they proudly share with perfect strangers that they are "one-fourth Thai." (My older daughter also sometimes mentions her Black granddad, hilariously adding to folks' confusion.)

According to the Pew Research Center, as of 2013, about nine million Americans chose two or more racial categories when asked about their race. No doubt there are more multiethnic folks than those who reported themselves on that survey. A study found that the number of Black-White biracial Americans doubled between 2000 and 2010.[18] And the 2020 Census results will likely show that trend to have continued or even increased. Mixed people have always been part of our country's story; now we are no longer seen as a subculture. We are no longer in the shadows.

Professor Robin DiAngelo acknowledges this shift and the changing nature of race, saying that using "the terms *white* and *people of color* to indicate the two macro-level, socially recognized divisions of racial hierarchy . . . [will lead to] collapsing a great deal of variation." She knows that because we multiethnic folks "challenge racial constructs and boundaries, [we] face unique challenges in a society in which racial categories have profound meaning."[19] When it comes to easy categories, there's no easy binary (*White versus person of color;* or *ally versus minority*) for most of us mixed folks to plug into. We just don't fit the system.

FORCED BINARY, OR CHECK ALL THAT APPLY?

The irony of trying to define the mixed experience is that we defy categorization. We know it's absurd to try to distill multiethnicity down to two distinctions; but as an initial starting point (and for the sake of sanity), we have to begin with something and then build from there. Some of us mixed folks readily identify with both categories, whereas others of us fit into only one, and others identify with every possible combination in-between.

It's a difficult distinction because some mixed folks are "simply" biracial, with one parent of one ethnic background and the other parent of another. Stu, who has a Black mom and a White dad, identifies more with descriptor one (having diversity within his family) than descriptor two (being a minority based on others' expectations), because his childhood home tended toward a monoethnic culture.[20] Cass, who has indigenous heritage from both parents, identifies less with definition one (diversity in family) and more with definition two (minority based on expectations) because he has Zuni ancestors on one side and Diné (Navajo) ancestors on the other (and White ancestry on both sides). He was raised within an overarching Native culture but isn't sure where he fits. However Stu, because he looks more like his Black mom, wrestles more with questions of how his experience in his family affects his internal identity than with issues of feeling like a mixed *other*. In contrast, Cass feels the strain of the expectations placed on him to be "fully" Zuni and "fully" Diné. His parents didn't dwell much on their tribal differences, but Cass feels the pressure to figure out his mixed identity in the context of his broader community.

Even for those who are multiethnic *without* White ancestry, in addition to the "usual" stress and experiences of being a *monoethnic* minority (especially as part of a displaced people group), there may be a sense of feeling unsure how to fit into multiethnic spaces. Brennan, who has Japanese and Chinese heritage, has fewer experiences that draw out the complications of multiethnicity, so he identifies less with descriptor one (diversity in family) and more with descriptor two (minority based on expectations). Brennan feels more internally secure in his Japanese and Chinese/Cantonese heritage than in how others see him, but in mixed spaces especially, he often feels "unseen [because of his] ambiguous Asian appearance." With his Japanese last name, he is most often assumed not to have other Asian ancestry. Sometimes he considers adding his Chinese names to better indicate his multiethnicity.

MIXED BLESSINGS

I wrestled for a while with the title *Mixed Blessing*. I wanted something as clever and uplifting as *Check All That Apply* (based on the progress from past census forms requiring "Other" or "None of the above" into the joy of being able to "Check all that apply" on the 2000 census).[21] We multiethnic folks know that one word or phrase can't sum us up, but *mixed* is once again gaining traction. As terms like *biracial* have necessarily given way to *multiracial* and then *multiethnic*, we've learned the value of affirming our dignity by choosing how to reference ourselves.

Sometimes I use the term *multiethnic* as an important way to indicate how we straddle two or more different worlds. I also sometimes refer to us as "people of multiethnicity" to honor the fact that we are indeed people of color who experience life in a distinct way due to our ethnicity. Some of us have chosen to breathe new life into the idea of multiethnicity by reclaiming previously derogatory words like *mixed* and making them our own.

Mixed has a complicated history and can conjure up images of livestock breeding and blood quantum, as author Randy Woodley explains,[22] with all their dehumanizing, polarizing, and violent implications. Being mixed teaches us that matters are rarely as mutually exclusive as they may seem, and even as we struggle over defining terms, *mixed* highlights how ambiguity is a large part of our multiethnic experience. I choose to reject the word's historical connotations. I don't allow the term—and thus myself—to uphold the false idea of the purity of whiteness, which implies people of color are sub-human animals to be bred. (I haven't met anyone who is working on rehabilitating the term *half-breed* yet!)

If you don't want to refer to yourself as mixed, that's okay too. The practice of reclamation is rooted in the right to identify our own selves, Elizabeth Sung reminds us,[23] to simultaneously humbly and proudly wear a mantle that was given by others for evil but that God intends for good. Each of us gets to choose words that best describe us and our current experiences. And our identity and story will shift over time from one thing to another, and sometimes back again.

While there are problems involved in any term, I find that *mixed* identifies my current experience best. Both in its positives and negatives, being mixed is not a perfect blending, not the utopian melting pot. It's a "mixed bag," and I often feel "mixed up." My ethnicity is indeed a "mixed blessing," and I sometimes feel like quite the pariah in "mixed company." But I do really value the ambiguity of *mixed*—the freedom to define it for myself and not to be limited to others' views of who they want me to be. I love the freedom to see myself as God sees me, in all my diversity.

MULTIETHNIC GROUPS, MIXED INDIVIDUALS

I also like that *mixed* has mostly fallen out of use to describe groups, so many of us people of multiethnicity are choosing to use it to describe ourselves as individuals. When we say something about a "multiethnic group," most monoethnic folks assume that means a group made up of a variety of monoethnic individuals, forgetting that we multiethnic folks even exist. *Mixed* pushes back on the idea that monoethnicity is the norm.

Societally, choosing to identify as a mixed person is also on the rise. For the most part, colorblindness as a virtue is out. We've moved past the 1990s' ideal and have realized that, as theologian Sarah Shin tells us, "colorblindness, though well intentioned, is inhospitable. Colorblindness assumes that we are similar enough and that we all only have good intentions, so we can avoid our differences."[24] But we have to ask if multiethnicity is the new colorblindness. Mixed people are increasingly in vogue, especially in the realm of advertising. "Sex sells" is a standby of the marketing world; apparently beige sells too.

While I agree that multiethnicity can be used as a mere marketing tactic, I also believe that we mixed folks can lead the way in being "color brave," as finance executive Mellody Hobson coined the phrase in her 2014 TED Talk. Rather than trying to ignore our differences, we can face reality head on and "become comfortable with being uncomfortable."[25] If there's one thing that we people of multiethnicity are practiced at, it's figuring out how to be at ease in uneasy situations, often ones which are triggered by our appearance and readily apparent differences.

Popular figures like Meghan Markle, Jason Momoa,[26] and Halle Berry are unabashedly multiethnic and have a range of different thoughts on what that means to them.[27] Some folks have even chosen to embrace the "one-drop rule,"[28] identifying with their Black ancestors and redeeming a previously negative structure. The beauty of diversity for us mixed folks is that everyone's multiethnic story is different.

Given our country's racial history, former president Barack Obama chooses to self-identify as Black *without* downplaying his White mother or denying his third-culture upbringing. Actor Chloe Bennet, upon realizing that her last name, Wang, was leading to her being typecast, chose to use another surname (quite common for actors). What's significant is that she chose her Chinese father's first name as her new last name, not her White mother's surname. She wanted to honor her heritage but not be limited by the stereotyping of Asians in Hollywood.[29]

Many popular figures are openly mixed, and discuss how their mixed ancestry has formed their identity and impact. In the same vein as Jason Momoa, Halle Berry, and Chloe Bennet, actors Dwayne "The Rock" Johnson, Rashida Jones, Keanu Reeves, Henry Golding, Chrissy Teigen, and Cameron Diaz talk about their mixed ancestry with fans and in interviews. Along the lines of Barack Obama's lead, politicians such as Kamala Harris and Tammy Duckworth are very open about their mixed ethnicity. Singers Shakira, Mariah Carey, and Ne-Yo have mixed ethnicity that they incorporate into their music. Actor Tracee Ellis Ross has developed a line of mixed haircare products, and actor Taye Diggs wrote a children's book entitled *Mixed Me*. There are many of us mixed folks, both famous and non, who are choosing to be "color brave"—to push into our ethnicity and pursue wholeness.

BUT WHAT ABOUT EUROPEAN AMERICANS?

There will no doubt be those who ask the question, "What about European Americans? What about those with Irish,

Italian, or Jewish heritage who were once considered minorities in America?" I won't say it's a *fair* question, but I will take
a second to address it. Looking at the distinctions I've offered,
there may indeed be some connection to both. Such a person
may feel some disconnect internally and when among others.
But the lack of minority status—not even the "model minority" perpetual-foreigner status that so affects Asian
Americans—is the key difference. If these mixed conversations bless majority-culture people and encourage them to
look more into their heritage, wonderful. But the very real
discriminations faced by many European immigrants are in
the past, with little to no current repercussions.

For White folks who "legally" immigrated and have suc-
cessfully integrated into the dominant White culture, there
is no lasting legacy upon them like the weight that is on
people of color in the United States today. The history of
human-stealing inherent in slavery, the land-stealing from
indigenous peoples, or the citizenship-stealing against Asian,
Latinx, and other immigrants is why the "people of color"
category is so necessary. Yes, there is grief when we think
about the discriminations of the past, about cultures and traditions that were lost, and about assimilation into acceptable
blandness. And there is great value for all folks in learning
more about their ethnic heritage, because one of the greatest
lies sown is that there are White folks and then there are
"ethnic" people. As Efrem Smith writes, "The fact is that all
Whites have an ethnic identity and heritage: Irish, British,
Danish, German, and so on. It is important for Whites to
engage their heritages to be able to find their rightful place
within a post-White, multiethnic community."[30] It is indeed

grievous to think about how "different White ethnic immigrant groups—Italians, Poles, Irish, and Jews—were marginalized or discriminated against because of their backgrounds" (even as they "found advantage in downplaying or even negating those identities").[31]

As DNA tests have become popular, many people are starting to understand that their heritage is rooted in more than their US ancestors. For some White folks, learning more about their family history can lead to a greater sympathy for and understanding of people of color. This can be valuable in enhancing communication. But for others, it may further entrench the idea of something other than whiteness being "exotic," which can further the false notion that White folks are also multiethnic. This false narrative can be uniquely difficult for us mixed folks whose experiences are directly affected by our embodied ethnic diversity—rather than being some novel footnote from the distant past.

It's important to draw lines of distinction, not to keep others out but to ensure that there's room for those of us who need and deserve this mixed space. It's hard to hear the voices of the marginalized when there are privileged voices shouting a very different message.

THE OTHER *OTHERS*

I do want to say that we honor monoethnic siblings who are transracially adopted and those in mixed "blended" families. Those who have vitiligo and albinism can empathize with being the *other* and with fighting against colorism on multiple fronts. Those third-culture folks who grew up in other countries and cultures can also empathize with our mixed experience. All these siblings are welcome in their beauty and joy, their tiredness and doubts. But as we invite these folks to sit at our table and rest a spell—to sit with us at the feet of Jesus—we do so in hopes that they will be encouraged to also gather at their own tables, in their own unique communities.

DEFINING TERMS, DEFINING OURSELVES

It can be wearying to not fit in. Keren, who is Black and White, says that when it comes to the "What are you?" guessing game, everyone assumes she is "everything except what I actually am!"—a lament many of us share. People ask if she's Latina, Middle Eastern, even Filipina, which makes her feel unseen even while she's stared at. Niki, who is Latina and White, mourns that monoethnic "people just assume that you're one of them. I'm not. I'm more than that; I'm other than that." Since we naturally push back against people's assumptions, we mixed folks can really benefit from clear ways to express ourselves.

As human beings created in the image of God, we have the right to be treated as such. As believers in Christ, though, and citizens of a "first shall be last" kingdom, we give up our rights. In so doing, we're bestowed with the right to call Jesus friend, to call God our father, and to call on the Holy Spirit to indwell us. Thus our right to dignity is anchored in Christ, not in ourselves. When we understand this, we can use things like the "Bill of Rights for Racially Mixed People" by author Maria P. P. Root in a way that is honoring to the Lord. In the same ways that monoethnic folks are able to define themselves and rise above expectations, so are we mixed people.

I have the right
> not to justify my existence in this world
>
> not to keep the races separate within me
>
> not to be responsible for people's discomfort with my physical ambiguity
>
> not to justify my ethnic legitimacy

I have the right
> to identify myself differently than strangers expect me to identify
>
> to identify myself differently than how my parents identify me
>
> to identify myself differently than my brothers and sisters
>
> to identify myself differently in different situations

I have the right
> to create a vocabulary to communicate about being multiracial
>
> to change my identity over my lifetime—and more than once
>
> to have loyalties and identify with more than one group of people
>
> to freely choose whom I befriend and love[32]

As we read this "bill of rights," we may find ourselves comforted, alarmed, confused, or even in total disagreement. I encourage us all to sit with the joy or the lament stirred up by such a bold proclamation. Though the story of Christianity is the laying down of our rights, we do have the right to approach the God of the universe on his throne and to ask him to show us what is healthy for us in seeking to be respected.

As we move from the more foundational aspects of being mixed to the nuanced stories of being mixed, we can trust that God will speak to us, no matter how still and small his voice may seem. He lovingly created us and he won't abandon us. As we see in the story of Hagar in the wilderness, who is the mother of a mixed child, it is El Roi (Gen 16:13, Heb. אֵל רֳאִי)—the God who *sees*—who has created and continues to sustain us mixed folks.

CHAPTER TWO

Multiethnicity 102

The Story of Being Mixed

Take a tray.
Receive food.
Sit.

On one side
of the bright, noisy room,
light skin.
Other side,
dark skin.

Both laughing, chewing,
as if it never occurred
to them
someone medium
would show up.

THANHHA LAI, FROM "BLACK AND WHITE AND YELLOW AND RED"[1]

ISHANI IS SOUTH ASIAN AND BRITISH, as well as being a second-generation American. When asked if she'd like to share anything regarding her experience of ethnicity and culture, her response highlighted the complications of not fitting one category. She said that just thinking about the question "made me really tired . . . this question is so loaded . . . I know that doesn't really answer the question but just expresses how tiresome these conversations can be."

I completely resonate with her statement. At the end of a full day spent with students and faculty, or playing with my kids, I may enjoy watching a sitcom or two: most of my favorites feature minority families who are (hilariously and authentically) wrestling with issues of race, multiethnicity, and multiculturalism. But after a long day of thinking about issues of mixed identity, my brain is very, very tired. Watching them feels more like work than R&R. I often have to resort to watching low-stakes, nonpolitical, almost "post-racial" British cooking shows instead—ones that are whimsical and inoffensively bland.

Moving beyond foundational issues of multiethnicity and pushing into our real, lived experiences of being mixed can be overwhelming. There can be both community and conflict, insight and alienation, as our varying identities interact with each other. Further complicating the definition of mixed ethnicity are things like intersectionality, multi*culturalism*, and code-switching. It's okay to rest when we need to so that we can have the energy to dive back in later. We are not driven by rigid standards of identity formation; we are empowered by the Holy Spirit to rest in the Lord.

THE "NU MATH" OF MULTIETHNICITY: INTERSECTIONALITY

Intersectionality—the ways in which our various identities influence and enhance each other[2]—can be at the core of our weariness. All humans experience exponential *othering*, both in terms of gender *and* race, or age *and* socioeconomic status, or sexuality *and* ethnicity, etc. Being a minority and being mixed do not operate independently of each other, but rather in tandem, each one adding to the other's layers of complexity. In terms of mathematics, the multiple identities of mixed folks do not work linearly, with simple 1+1=2 addition. Rather, the joy and the weariness are both affected exponentially, in more of a 2 x 2 x 2 fashion. Certainly our weariness can't be reduced to mere mathematical terms, but it's helpful to acknowledge and visualize some of the ways that mixed identity is complex.

Our self-perspective changes over time. Especially for us mixed folks, this can happen frequently and fluidly. As we think through our varying identities, multiethnic identity may seem to be mathematically impossible: 1+1 does not equal 1, and even more, ½ x ½ actually equals ¼, which is that much further from our goal of "wholeness." Analogies aside, even thinking about the complexities of multiethnic identity is exhausting, much less living it. Add to that the issues with being identified by others on their terms, not our own, and it's no surprise that so many of us feel weary and in need of rest.

THE MESTIZO/A EXPERIENCE OF IN-BETWEEN

When governmental forms, such as the national census, still define race and ethnicity differently than other social and political systems, it can be confusing. Pew Research staff Ana Gonzalez-Barrera and Mark Hugo Lopez acknowledge this confusion, even among those who identify as Hispanic and especially among multiethnic folks. "A new Pew Research Center survey of multiracial Americans finds that, for two-thirds of Hispanics, their Hispanic background *is* a part of their racial background—not something separate. This suggests that Hispanics have a unique view of race that doesn't necessarily fit within the official U.S. definitions."[3] For many, the heart of being Hispanic or Latino/a is the *mestizo/a* ("mixed," also written as *mestizx*)[4] experience, even as the group definition of mestizx grows and changes over time.

For those of us mixed individuals who have Latinx heritage, there can be an added dimension. Alanah, who is Latina and White, helpfully explains that in her experience, "Latinx and Hispanic are only *cultural* identifiers in the United States because in countries throughout Latin America, we do have a *racial* category for Brown Latinx people who are mixed indigenous, European, and potentially African. There are Asian Latinx people, Black Latinx, White Latinx, and not all of those people are 'mixed' necessarily—they are the race that they identify with situated in Latin America." Self-identity is key to defining both race and culture.

Another article on the Census Bureau website further clarifies: "The data on race are based on self-identification and the categories on the form generally reflect a social definition of race. The categories are not an attempt to define race biologically, anthropologically, or genetically."

Well that, as the cliché goes, is as "clear as mud." In fact, the idea of multiracial people "muddying the waters" has often been used as a way to demean both nonwhite and mixed folks, with the implication that the "White race" is best left pure. But the presence of God's good gift of melanin is *not* what's mucking things up. It's the absence of humility and community—two attributes we all must strive for. We mixed folks know this struggle well.

LIVING IN THE EMBODIED AND COGNITIVE DISSONANCE

Adding to the uniquely confusing nature of having mixed ethnicity is the fact that most of us come from two or more ethnic heritages with historical and current animosity. This means simultaneously being the oppressor *and* the oppressed. For many of us mixed folks, our visible physical characteristics—our phenotypes—don't fit the cultural norms that divide people into "red and yellow, black and white."[5] So we embody slaves *and* masters, colonizers *and* indigenous people, vulnerable immigrants *and* privileged gatekeepers, all in the face of one person. We see the hostility of centuries every time we look in the mirror.

For those of us whose ethnicities seem more compatible to a monoethnic worldview or can be grouped under a larger region or people group (such as "Asia" or "Native Americans"), we may still experience dissonance based on other characteristics, like styles of dress or speech. As scientists explain, the human brain automatically (and often subconsciously) categorizes the distinctive features of the people around us.[6] So visible racial and ethnic characteristics make a difference in how all people see others. These implicit biases do not stop with phenotype, however. They also manifest in how our cultural characteristics are perceived.

Body types, facial markers, and cultural representations also make a difference in how we mixed folk see ourselves. For many of us, the dilemma is not just how to identify in relation to others, but also how to identify ourselves internally. When we have different (seemingly competitive) communication styles, cultural values, priorities, etc., within our person, it can be difficult to figure out where competition ends and we begin. And regardless of whether or not there is any history of animosity between those different cultures, for us mixed folks there can be a continual sense of disconnect, uncertainty, and loss. Without specific spiritual growth and healing, there is rarely a sense of harmony or unity that integrates all parts of the self fully. We mixed folks live in dissonance.

MULTIETHNICITY AND MULTICULTURALISM

To some, multiculturalism seems to be outside the scope of our conversation. Monoethnic folks, while not a visual monolith, usually can identify with their culture through their ethnicity. But in some ways, multiculturalism is the heart of the matter. In terms of an "are you in or are you out?" dichotomy of group belonging, appearance is not all that matters. I've noticed that being accepted as "culturally half-Black" can be predicated (perhaps subconsciously) on the fact that I'm also genetically mixed. I think it comes from folks knowing that although I do have a lot of White privilege, I also understand the minority experience in America. I'm not "colorblind," and I'm not content with the status quo. Rather than being fully vested in White fragility, being mixed means that I long for change but also may be more likely to understand the dangers of a "White savior complex."

There's something sacred about sharing our culture with another. It's a holy thing to call someone else "one of us," thus making ourselves vulnerable to attack from those who were once outside the camp and are now in it. It helps to know that former *others* understand some measure of the discrimination and exclusion we've experienced. We need reassurance that they don't think they have all the answers. When majority-culture White people enter a minority space, they change it. The dichotomy reawakens: the haves and the have-nots. Though none of us is one-dimensional, the tone shifts to a reminder that there are those who would say that we are. To push back against this dynamic, we continue to tell our story, as exhausted as we are. We lean into the ways in which we disrupt norms. We provoke questions, and we ask questions in return.

ALLEGIANCES AND CODE-SWITCHING

Minorities in a majority-culture world understand the need to present differently in different situations so as to navigate different cultural norms and to function within the dominant culture of our society. For example, those folks from Spanish-speaking households may feel undue pressure to speak English in the United States without the trills of a Spanish accent. Or people of color or recent immigrants, despite their own cultural norms of schedule fluidity, may work hard to follow the Western system that sees punctuality as a moral imperative to communicate respect and value.

Despite a majority culture which requires others to adapt to its own norms, *code-switching*[7] (shifting behavior according to different circumstances) is often seen as negative. And it can certainly be awkward or forced for monoethnic, *majority-culture* folks: We've all seen people who try too hard to be part of a culture not their own, putting on affectations in style of dress and music choices. We've all felt the awkwardness of seeing White folks act in unfamiliar or stereotypical ways in their attempt to fit in with "ethnic" folks. For the monoethnic person, whether within minority, majority, or both cultures, code-switching comes with a lot of baggage and issues. For us mixed folks, code-switching can be a unique minefield.

And being mixed can actually require almost constant code-switching; when I am with different family or community members, my speech patterns and word choices naturally shift, as well as my body language and mannerisms. Our instinctive habit to present differently within different communities can be perceived by monoethnic people of color as being a "sell-out" to the majority culture. If we (knowingly or unknowingly) suppress an accent or speech pattern when talking to someone of the majority culture, we may be accused of being pretentious.

If one of us mixed folks who has both African American and European roots chooses to use the highly enunciated dialect of majority-culture American English, there may be shameful accusations of trying to "act White." Paradoxically, even when slipping into familiar linguistic habits of minority-culture upbringing (or exploring aspects of unfamiliar culture), we may be seen as committing cultural appropriation in using the more fluid dialect of stereotypical African American English. We mixed folks can offend multiple cultures in multiple ways, all at the same time, merely in an effort to be fully embodied in our multiethnicity.

It is indeed harmful and unjust when privileged majority-culture folks take ideas, styles, or cultural artifacts from another people group without giving appropriate credit, without understanding the nuances of that culture, and for their own consumption and benefit.[8] The dilemma, for us mixed folks, is being a walking cultural appropriation. According to social norms, a part of us is always appropriating culture from other parts of us. We are always colonizing and being colonized; always offending and being offended; always stealing and being stolen from.

GOING ON THE OFFENSE

We mixed people indeed have the unique ability to offend all parties involved. Trying to intentionally avoid this is also exhausting, in large part because code-switching is sometimes purposeful but most often instinctual. When we lean into one aspect of our various mixed identities, it can be offensive to others as we modify our styles of dress, behavior, and even speech patterns to match internal and external expectations. In reality, all humans code-switch: we "dress up" for special events or "dress down" for leisure activities. We speak more formally when in court or at a solemn occasion, and we use casual words with friends and family. Many folks have what I like to call a "phone and prayer voice" when they become more businesslike and more soothingly cordial.

Monoethnic minorities certainly code-switch as a survival mechanism, adapting their mannerisms to better communicate with and be accepted by majority-culture institutions. For us mixed folks, however, there's a weariness in the need to code-switch, as we adjust to differing cultures in our homes and other places that should be restful. Many of us feel the burden even when we're alone, in our own heads. We wonder who we *really* are and worry that we're merely an amalgamation of parts, not a whole person. Left to my own devices, I'm not always sure what styles of dress and speech are most comfortable for me. So even when I'm alone, I feel unsure of my motivations and whether I'm being genuine or not. By myself, even small decisions regarding behavior and appearance can feel paralyzing, so I often just give up and take a nap. It may not be the most healthy coping mechanism, but it's also part of self-care, I tell myself.

BEING "OUTSIDE THE BOX"

Many of us mixed folks wish that others could tell our ethnicities (in all their complexity) at first glance. Whether we appear monoethnic or "ambiguous," we don't want to have to explain our ethnicity (and thus ourselves) over and over again. We resent those who assume we're one thing or another. And yet we find ourselves doing the same thing with other mixed folks. In the same vein of being both oppressors and the oppressed, colonizers and the colonized, we are the unseen and those who do not see fully.

We also forget the complexity of multiethnicity beyond our own experience. In the survey I wrote, I asked mixed folks to check all that applied in a list of ethnic and racial identities. Someone graciously pointed out that I'd left out siblings with Middle Eastern roots. At first I was content to let them identify in the overall "Asian" category, but the more I thought about it, the more I realized I needed to make a change. I apologized, reworked the survey, and was grateful for a reminder that these questions are intricate and complicated. More importantly, I needed the reminder that they matter to specific people who have specific experiences of being unseen and left out.

But being outside of societal norms and expectations is not always a bad thing; in some ways it's a gift. When we mixed folks tell our stories, we showcase reconciliation, not least because we're willing to be honest. We're honest about our pain. We run to the Father, and we depend on the Holy Spirit. We admit that we bear grief in our bodies. We live in the "here and not yet." In all this, we pick up our cross daily and imitate Jesus. And we come together as a community. This is the gospel at work.

DIVERSE UNITY, HOPEFUL LAMENT

Being honest about grief can foster places of connection, belonging, and rest for us mixed folks. As Soong-Chan Rah explains, to avoid hollow triumphalism, we must not fall into the trap that plagues so much of the White American church.[9] As we examine the stories that the Bible tells, and as we seek to locate our own stories within biblical context, "to only have a theology of celebration at the cost of the theology of suffering is incomplete. The intersection of the two threads provides the opportunity to engage in the fullness of the gospel message. Lament and praise must go hand in hand."[10] Before other folks can love us well, they must listen to and lament with us. Before we can love ourselves well, we must do the same.

When we believers take our views of others not as gospel truth but as a good starting point, we're able to seek the mind of Christ and to see others through his eyes. As we seek to know what God says about ethnicity and how he sees us mixed folks, we can rely on eternal gospel truths: the goodness of God and his love for all of us. When we interact with Jesus' teachings from our multiethnic perspective, we're honoring the *imago Dei* in us all. To be flexible and humble in hearing others' perspectives is a healthy refusal to choose sides, a forceful denial of the lie that we must all be homogeneous to be a family. This is the essence of being multiethnic, the heart of being mixed.

CHAPTER THREE

Rejecting Stereotypes, Understanding Prototypes, Embracing Stories

In her TED Talk "The Danger of a Single Story," author Chimamanda Ngozi Adichie illustrates how people tend to reduce others to just one narrative. When discussing one of her novels with an American student, he commented that it's sad Nigerian men are abusive, like the character in her novel. Her response was priceless: "I told him that I had just read a novel called *American Psycho* and that it was such a shame that young Americans were serial murderers."

Though she humorously clapped back in a "fit of mild irritation" she adds, "It would never have occurred to me to think that just because I had read a novel in which a character was a serial killer that he was somehow representative of all Americans. This is not because I am a better person than that student, but because of America's cultural and economic power I had many stories of America." Getting to the heart of racism, colorism, and other prejudicial -*ism*s, she shows how "power is the ability not just to tell the story of another person, but to make it the definitive story of that person."[1]

We're all guilty of this in different situations and with different people. Sometimes it's out of malice, but perhaps more often it's out of misguided sympathy, misplaced loyalty, or just being misinformed. Our ability to empathize with people is often directly proportional to how well we understand them. When we don't do the work of really seeing and hearing people, we can miss them entirely, all the while thinking we've understood them.

We reduce people to a single story, despite conventional wisdom (and political correctness) telling us to avoid stereotyping people based on their race. However, as we mixed folks know, it's not so cut-and-dried. To avoid the enticing ideal of colorblindness, we must acknowledge—and then *celebrate*—differences between people. Though we must resist judgments against people based on their appearance, it's difficult to set aside first impressions and to refrain from defining people based on our perception of them. As Christena Cleveland explains, our brains naturally sort the world around us to "conserve valuable cognitive resources by categorizing . . . to help us interact with an individual and predict his or her behavior. Categorizing can be helpful in many ways." We save time by creating larger categories for individual objects. Imagine if we had to relearn what a fork is (as opposed to a spoon) every time we ate.

But this innate habit can also do great harm. Cleveland continues, "In our haste to conserve mental energy we often erect divisions out of thin air by grouping people into smaller homogenous categories."[2] We instinctively judge individuals based on the stereotypes of their ethnicity—and usually for the worse. Police brutality against minorities—even young children of color—has proven that.[3] It takes a lot of conscious antiracism work to overcome our ingrained prejudices.[4]

A WHOLE SPECTRUM OF PEOPLE

In the face of human nature and systemic injustice, what can we do? How do we battle racism and colorism when they're part of the air we breathe? Even those who tout their lack of negative stereotypes still don't realize a problem with lumping individuals into one group. For example, the "model minority" myth[5] posits that all Asian Americans are inherently smart (especially in math) and hard-working. This myth is dehumanizing on several levels. In making Asian Americans an "acceptable" monolithic group, it turns "model citizen" Asian Americans into a prop that entrenches negative stereotypes of groups such as African Americans. Trying to break these cultural norms is exhausting and incites further judgment from the majority culture.

While American majority culture may consider "smart" and "hard-working" to be positive characteristics, putting any kind of preconceived notion on another person is harmful. *Positive* stereotypes are still stereotypes. When we stereotype people, we're guilty of putting our judgments on them, thus limiting authentic interactions with them. It's difficult to have a real relationship with a caricature instead of a flesh-and-blood, image-bearing human. And that's just in terms of monoethnicity. Once we multiethnic folks are added to the mix, we bear the brunt of further White pushback for breaking the stereotypes that have been placed on us.

Rather than trafficking in stereotypes, a valuable spiritual exercise is to look at prototypes. Consider researcher Eleanor Rosch's prototype theory, which originated in cognitive psychology: "Rather than requiring all necessary and sufficient conditions, prototype theory requires possession of some but not all common qualities for membership in a category."[6] *Stereotypes* focus on the lie that all people in a certain category are completely alike, but *prototypes* acknowledge similarities in certain people without locking any one person into every aspect of their culture.

Prototypes are characteristics generally associated with a culture, ethnicity, or region, and they can include types of communication, cultural artifacts, and styles of dress, music, art, and so on. Prototype theory allows for individual differences within a culture, instead of stereotypes that assume certain characteristics always apply to everyone within that group.

For example, a prototype of Greek culture is that family is paramount, people are loud, and food is plentiful. This is certainly not true of all Greek folks, but it's part of the national and cultural ethos. For Southern folks in the United States, a prototype is that they are hospitable, indirect communicators who love their college football. Again, this isn't true of all Southerners, but it's a generally accepted—and celebrated— prototype. A fair prototype of Thai culture is that the people are Buddhist/animist, love spicy foods, and have an affection for foreign tourists. This is generally true of Thai folks—and it's even promoted by their tourism department—but it's not true of all Thais.

The distinction between stereotypes and prototypes is sticky, but it lies in the wording and in our attitude.

Stereotypes are fixed in place and unyielding (literally, from the Greek *stereos*, meaning "solid").[7] Prototypes are, by their very nature, only the starting point in a discussion (from the Greek *prototypon*, meaning "first or primitive"),[8] not the ending. A prototype is a general observation to foster new insights and interactions. When we allow our attitude about a culture—and by extension, about individual people—to be shaped by flexible ideas, not rigid preconceptions, we can appreciate the prototypical aspects of a culture and then listen to people's stories to learn more about them as individuals.

Acknowledging general prototypes instead of relying on entrenched stereotypes prevents us from treating an entire ethnic or cultural group as a monolith. Admitting that it's our *information* that is primitive—not the people we are observing—is an exercise in humility. Prototypes are generally positive (or at least neutral); stereotypes usually focus on our negative ideas. A harmful stereotype focuses on another culture's contrast to our own experience, which makes the other culture seem exotic, frightening, or just plain wrong. For example, some people from a quiet American family may perceive Greek folks as being too loud. But in holding on to that stereotype, they'll miss out in two ways: First, they won't learn about the beauty of a culture so different from their own. Second, they'll miss out on seeing the diversity within Greek culture, thus limiting healthy interactions with Greek individuals.

When I first moved to the Deep South ten years ago, I was at a loss culturally. I couldn't understand the give-and-take nature of indirect communication. I wondered, *If someone wants some sweet tea, why can't they just say so? Why the hemming and hawing?* I stubbornly clung to my own idea of hospitality ("Make yourself at home. Feel free to get anything you need!") and my tendency toward direct communication. It took a lot of repentance from me, as well as patience from my new community, for me move past my own preferences and my negative stereotypes of Southerners.

I needed to acknowledge the prototype of Southern hospitality—and not actively resist it—so I could find my own place in the story. And I needed to move past my judgment of it so I could see others in how they both aligned with and differed from the general cultural narrative.

A PEOPLE WITH A WHOLE SPECTRUM

For us mixed folks, our multiethnicity can complicate things. Negative or (supposedly) positive stereotypes can be harmful for people of monoethnicity, but they are also fraught for us people of multiethnicity. Because we have more than one ethnic identity, all of the negative assumptions are compounded, as are the positive expectations.

When I first visited Thailand, my family took a day trip to a *wat* (temple) in memory of my grandfather and to give gifts to the monks. I told my family I couldn't bow to the Buddha or offer prayers but I'd be honored to stand respectfully to the side. This was another of those foundational moments for me: I was keenly aware that I wasn't among the Thais, prostrate before the golden statue, rhythmically shaking prayer sticks. But I also wasn't with the other White tourists, taking pictures, pointing, and talking loudly. I wasn't merely a *farang* (foreigner) who was affectionately tolerated in that sacred space. I so longed to be *Thai* in that strange moment—but even if I had looked more

Asian or was a practicing Buddhist, I still wouldn't have fit in either category. I'd still have been an anomaly.

The term "heart language" is often used in missions to describe a person's first language, the one that was spoken at home. But for some of us mixed folks who grew up multilingual, there's more than one heart language, more than one reality that feels authentic to who we are. Steve, who identifies as "biracial White Latino," was visiting a Cuban American church and overheard two people talking. "This guy's White, but he's also Cuban," said one man to the other *en Español,* expecting Steve not to understand. But he did understand their Spanish (perhaps unfortunately, in that case). *Am I Latino enough?* Steve thought, echoing what many of us mixed folks feel. *Do I belong in this community, or am I just an outsider?* When folks perceive us as a contradiction in terms, we may feel like we are a nuisance at best, and at worst an interloper.

Kristina, who also has Latinx and White heritage, has had a similar experience of not belonging, but because she *doesn't* speak Spanish fluently. In middle school, she was required to take a test because the administration saw her Latinx last name. The test was entirely in Spanish, and she was very embarrassed, realizing that "I didn't know this language that I was supposed to know." She was expected to need English as a Second Language training, all based on her last name. The school's well-intentioned racial stereotyping was no doubt a help to some of her classmates, but for Kristina (and others who didn't fit the mold), it was traumatizing. "Whenever I hear Spanish, I still get a little anxious," she confesses, reliving the pain of not meeting expectations all over again.

For many of us who weren't raised to speak a language other than English, this can be a source of pain and embarrassment. Because I was not raised to speak Thai, learning that beautiful tonal language as an adult has been difficult. My children are picking things up much more quickly and retaining them much better than I am—but they aren't learning Thai from infancy, from their parent. It won't be a heart language for them in the way that English is, and that will be part of their struggle as they work to reconcile and embrace their multiethnicity.

In his book *When Half Is Whole*, Stephen Murphy-Shigematsu shares his own and others' multiethnic stories, particularly the expectations placed on them because of their appearance: some good, some bad, and most of them conflicting. One of the storytellers, Japanese and Norwegian Lane Hirabayashi, related that an elementary teacher asked him, "Will you stop squinting like that? What's the matter? Do you need glasses?" because the teacher assumed that he was White and merely squinting in an affected way. Hirabayashi added, "Later on, in high school, I was to hear the other story, the flipside of the Eurasian coin. The ex-army typing teacher would smile and greet me: 'Konnichiwa' he would say in some half-forgotten GI Japanese. . . . What could I have said that would have reflected my own feelings, or that would have unmasked his assumptions?"[9]

We mixed folks may fulfill the stereotypes of one ethnicity but not the other. Or we may confirm stereotypes of more than one ethnicity. Both from within and without, we have numerous expectations heaped upon us, and we're unable to fulfill them all (even if that were a healthy thing).

Add to that the expectations within families, and the situation is even more complex. A pair of siblings that has one parent who is prototypically Latina and another parent who is the epitome of American whiteness will experience the world differently, not only due to their mixed heritage but also due to their different skin tones and mannerisms. Though raised in the same household by the same two people, the different ways in which they reflect each parent will affect the assumptions and expectations that others place on each sibling.

If their appearance is very different, especially in terms of skin tone, hair, and other phenotypical markers, their experiences will likely be very different. Kristina has much lighter skin than her brother, especially in the summer; at a month-long leadership institute for college students, no one realized they were siblings. When invitations were issued to a breakout session for people of color, she was pleasantly surprised to be asked. And despite her brother having a more traditional Mexican appearance, both siblings were initially hesitant to attend the session. After discussing it together, her brother said—with equal parts silliness and seriousness in answer to whether they even qualified as people of color, "I think we count." Because the event organizers looked beyond the stereotypes of both a person of color and of a mixed person, and instead saw Kristina and her brother in their fullness, value and acceptance were communicated.

WE'RE HARDEST ON OURSELVES

In addition to societal and familial expectations are the expectations that we mixed people put on ourselves. Some of us try to fulfill everyone's desires for us, that we be "authentic" representatives of our ancestry. We may feel the need to represent all the beauty and goodness of our cultures while combating all their gross stereotypes. Even if we manage to pull it off, the strain can be difficult. While monoethnic minorities can feel pressure to represent their race well, we mixed people can feel the magnified pressure of doing justice to all parts of us. Add to that how each of our cultures expresses values in different ways, and you have the perfect recipe for the loneliness, fear, and exhaustion that many of us experience.

Even as we strive to reject the stereotypes of monoethnic cultures, we have our own unique struggles against stereotypes that are specific to multiethnicity. As we acknowledge some of the prototypical struggles for us mixed folks, it's important to push back against unhealthy expectations. We need to combat tropes that folks have of mixed people: the "tragic mulatto,"[10] the wandering *mestizo*, the lonely *hapa*, the bewildered "hybrid." Of course, the solution is not to pretend our multiethnicity doesn't exist. We don't wallow in our misery, but neither do we just shove it aside. Rather we step into it and watch God bring healing to difficult places.

Indeed, learning to make the best out of our situation and continuing to value oneself in the midst of ridicule or isolation is a key part of the minority experience in America. As a small taste of the holistic peace we're longing for, it's empowering to see marginalized people thrive in the face of adversity.

Let me state plainly that there is nothing inherently tragic about people of multiethnicity. No, there is something tragic about a world that thinks it's better off without us.

Theologian Brian Bantum, who identifies as Black and White, chose the title *Redeeming Mulatto* for his book that examines the important realities of Jesus' body in relation to his own multiethnic body. He wrote, "We must look to Jesus again and be confronted with his own impossibility and the possibilities he creates out of our lives and for our lives. We must see this mulatto Jesus as not only for a particular people, but we must begin to see how the mulatto Jesus stands before us to remake all people."[11]

Keren, who has learned much over many years of embracing her Black and White identity, says, "The stereotype of biracial people being confused and socially awkward has a long history. It's the stereotype that bothers me the most." As she battles against the stereotypes she encounters as a woman, Christian, mother, etc., the one she finds most frustrating and hurtful is others' assumption that she will be left out of racial and cultural groups because she is biracial. So part of her journey has been pushing into her multiethnicity, seeking to live out the joyful complexities for others to see. As is common among people of color, she knows that lament and rejoicing are not opposites. They have been intertwined throughout human history, as evidenced in the story of humanity that we see in the Bible.

The good news is that when we mixed folks feel comfortable embracing prototypes and rejecting stereotypes as we see fit, we can experience freedom. And as we continue to shake off the unreasonable expectations placed on us, we can walk with others in that journey. We can lead the way in affirming that humans are a product of our genetics and our upbringing *and also* of our own cultural choices. We have the privilege of telling others that we aren't here to live within the limitations set by them. We get to discover who *Jesus* has designed us to be, moment by moment. Within the bounds of biblical fidelity (something all people interpret through cultural lenses), we're free to hold up each prototypical habit and tendency to see if it fits us in that circumstance. As Paul encouraged in Colossians 2, instead of being constrained by a forced view of biblical culture, we have the freedom—in Christ—to explore all facets of our ethnic background.

CHEERFULLY DEFYING STEREOTYPES

Many of us mixed folks strive to embrace the complexity of ourselves and others, even in our weariness. Gabby, who identifies as Native and White, said, "I want people to see me as a complex individual, and I want to see others the same way." For her, it can be "strange identifying as Native and Christian. People assume I'm either White and Christian or Native and spiritual." She's able to break this stereotype—the lie, really— that only White folks are true Christians and that Native folks can't keep any of their tribal culture if they are to accept the gospel.

In her embodied multiethnicity, Gabby is a perfect example of an imperfect human who is figuring out what it means to follow Jesus, the perfect one. In the First Nations Version of the Bible, Jesus is called "Creator Sets Free," a beautiful antidote to majority-culture norms. In majority-culture ears, the name *Jesus* has lost much of its original meaning (coming from the Hebrew *Yehoshua*, and transliterated *Joshua*, meaning "the LORD saves" (יְהוֹשֻׁעַ, derived from the sacred name יהוה). But Gabby's mixed personhood, her refusal to settle for one perspective, is a reminder that Jesus is also not a single story; his name represents a diverse lineage.

Adam is Asian and White, with Chinese and mostly Polish heritage, but he also strongly identifies with cultures where he's lived: previously in New Mexico, and now in Hawai'i. When he read Chicana writer Gloria Anzaldúa's *Borderlands/ La Frontera: The New Mestiza*, he realized that his experiences in those borderland locales echoes his own journey as a multiethnic and multicultural person. His ability to appreciate multiple stories informs his ability to appreciate new cultures. His mixed identity is a source of strength to him, and he wishes that "others saw themselves and others more clearly." Adam appreciates that with a focus on "each individual's humanity, everyone and their origins become special and something to be celebrated."

When we embrace our mixed reality and all that it signifies, we can rise above what separates us and enjoy the diversity of the human experience. Contrary to the words of *The Incredibles'* evil genius, Syndrome, who shouts a very human truth—"When everyone's super, no one is"—the staggering, ridiculous, offensive truth of the gospel is that all image bearers are special and should be celebrated.

GIFTS WILLINGLY GIVEN, NOT
TREASURES WILLFULLY STOLEN

So, can all people assume whatever cultural norms they'd like, regardless of ethnic background?[12] Should this chameleon-like tendency of mixed folks be something to celebrate or to warn against? What about cultural appropriation? The answers here are complicated—and yet painfully simple.

Another contrast when exploring stereotypes and proto-types is the key difference between cultural *appropriation* and cultural *appreciation*. Unlike the Terms and Conditions fine print in the latest software upgrade, these details matter. Setting healthy boundaries is very important to a conversation by, about, and with mixed people. This is especially true when it comes to charges of cultural appropriation that we may have levied against us.

Cultural appropriation is stealing from another culture, making assumptions, and not appreciating nuance. When one culture—usually a dominant or privileged one—capitalizes on, mocks, or consumes a culture without giving credit, that's cultural appropriation—and it's dishonoring to the *imago Dei* in us all. Cultural appropriation goes hand in hand with the violent appropriation—the *theft*—of nonwhite bodies and their land, wealth, and other precious resources. These crimes have been committed throughout our country's bloody history, and even today, cultural appropriation is at every level of society—often where it's least expected.

During a trip to Disney World's EPCOT theme park, I experienced this on a very visceral level. The park is divided into several "countries," with the architecture, food, and landscape of each country represented. Actual citizens from each country also work there. As I wandered from the "Japan" area to the "Mexico" section, I saw a fair amount of both cultural appropriation and appreciation. On the appreciation side, many of the replica buildings, temples, statues, and other landmarks were beautifully done. I felt a sense of awe at seeing a slightly smaller—yet still impressive—Eiffel Tower in "France." I experienced some measure of tranquility while standing in a Zen garden in "China." The food in "Morocco" was delicious, and the streets of "England" were charming. I did enjoy it, and it made me long to visit each country in reality.

And yet, on the appropriation side, I was alarmed to see people buying cheap, Americanized trinkets from each country. There were plastic sombreros with Mickey ears in "Mexico," light-up katana swords in "Japan," and ubiquitous Disney logo–emblazoned beer mugs in "Germany," all of which ironically bore a "MADE IN CHINA" sticker. This reduced each culture to its basest stereotypes, the epitome of consuming a culture without really knowing it. A profit was being made through stereotypes.

In contrast, cultural appreciation is valuing, affirming, and striving to support a culture *with all its nuance and complications.* Someone practicing cultural appreciation seeks to respectfully explore and understand the prototypes of a culture, those overarching narratives that set a culture apart from other cultures. This isn't usually the easiest path, especially when the values of other cultures seem to contradict our own. But it's one of the greatest commandments that we love people as complex human beings, not as conveniences to be used or threats to be avoided. And we mixed folks tend to know how to live in this nuance.

When we stereotype people and cultures, we assume we have all the information we need to know about the *other.* Where there may be a basic level of appreciation for a person or a culture, it's actually a false appreciation built on pretense. But when we start with what we know of a culture's prototypes and then push beyond them, we're admitting that our information is woefully incomplete. Rather than making assumptions based on hearsay or lack of interaction, a person who resists stereotyping and instead consults a prototype can see both commonalities and differences as a starting point for mutual growth.

When we realize how little we actually understand others, the Holy Spirit can guide us in knowing those cultures and people better. More importantly, when we use information as a starting point, not a stopping point, it's possible to truly delight in people and all their nuances. When we traffic in stereotypes, we're bound to judge others and to seek to avoid them. But when we use prototypes as a springboard, we'll have the opportunity to embrace others, to learn from and alongside them.

BALANCING CREDIT WHERE CREDIT IS DUE

Cultural appreciation is not merely giving credit where credit is due, though that's part of it. It's also about giving honor and receiving gifts gratefully. Those learning to enjoy a cultural artifact from a person of another ethnicity must be careful to acknowledge the intrinsic value of the art, music, literature, and so on. They need to make it clear that they are being gifted with this cultural artifact and that they want to learn more about that culture through their experience and by listening to the stories of those within the culture.

By the nature of our ancestry, we mixed folks don't need to acknowledge our experiences as a gift from outside our culture but as part of our heritage from within. And though we may look one way or the other in terms of our phenotype, we have a right to as much or as little of our ethnicity as we see fit. Our ancestors' blood flows in our veins. Our forebears' struggles and triumphs have formed our character. Our family of origin's reality has created each of us as a distinct person. And yet, with mixed ethnicity (and often in crosscultural/ transracial adoption or blended families), it's not as simple as proclaiming that truth and moving on.

Even if we aren't actually appropriating our own culture, we may be seen as doing that. We multiethnic folks know that there's a lot at stake in how we present ethnically, how we represent our culture. When I put in my largest hoop earrings (prototypically favored by African American women), I'm doing so because I think they look beautiful, and it makes me think of my Black family members' beauty and strength. I'm not doing it to "fit in" or to try to be something I'm not; I'm doing it because it reminds me of my auntie and cousin.

HEIGHTENED AWARENESS, CULTURAL APPRECIATION

But I'm also aware that I'm "only" culturally Black (and "half," at that!), and in my genetic Asian-White diversity, I present as mostly White. So I need to tread carefully when I interact with others. Whether I'm wearing my Black Lives Matter shirt or Thai silk skirt, I'm very conscious of the contrast with my appearance. Thai silk has a distinctive pattern, and I know that though I have ancestors who walked the ground of Thailand and wore similar patterns, I don't look very Thai. When visiting Thailand, I'm well aware that I look more like a tourist than a local, and I'm painfully conscious that because I was raised solely in the United States, the vast majority of Thai culture is foreign to me. What then? Do I push blindly ahead, potentially offending and confusing others? Or do I fold up and lay aside that part of myself, surrendering to the idea that I just don't qualify?

That's the pain—but also the privilege—of being mixed. Rather than being a walking cultural appropriation, I can strive to be a walking cultural *appreciation*, showing what it can look like to receive cultural gifts graciously from within and without. People don't usually question *why* monoethnic folks have a right to dress, to act, or to engage others according to their ethnic prototypes, even while judging those cultural norms. But in our multiethnicity, we're often suspect. Even more painful, this suspicion is in the face of the fact that we may have done more hard work to learn about our history and culture than folks who've had monoethnic access to cultural norms. We mixed folks have to think things through deeply, to ask a lot of personal questions about authenticity.

Sherrene, who is Indian American, asks a very poignant question: "How do I know what parts of my Indian culture are biblical? How can I see that part of myself without White normativity confusing the issue?" In many ways, the answer lies in the question. Monoethnic minority folks know what it's like to have their nonwhite culture placed against the measuring stick of "biblical culture," while many White folks just assume that their norms in worship and life *are* biblical. As Sherrene works through being married to a White man, parenting her son (an adoptee from India), and being an outspoken minority in her church, she has to ask herself a lot of these questions. She doesn't have the "luxury" of assuming that her default culture is the healthy one.

Sherrene's multiethnic and multicultural family has to do the good work of questioning what is "from God" and who are "false prophets" (1 Jn 4:1). Their conversations aren't theoretical, pie-in-the-sky fancies. They know "every spirit that acknowledges that Jesus Christ has come in the flesh is from God" (1 Jn 4:2), and that the flesh Christ came in is multiethnic and multicultural, not White.

We mixed folks with obviously European ancestry have to do the almost constant work of parsing out whether our White normativity is informing our view of our minority selves. And for those of us who are mixed with an all-minority ethnicity, the White normativity of the Western church still looms large. Being a "full" minority also means sorting out multiple ethnicities in contrast to each other. Whether we look more like one ethnicity or are phenotypically mixed in appearance (that dreaded yet coveted "ambiguity"), we deserve to be honored in our choices. It's our right to choose how we engage our ethnicity—and all the prototypes associated with it, including how it manifests in our appearance.

WHOLE PEOPLE, WHOLLY RELIANT ON JESUS

We are whole people, and we deserve to be seen that way. Embracing all of ourselves is a process, not a goal, and we multiethnic folks know this journey well. When the world—and even those of us within the mixed community—can stop *insisting* that multiethnic folks identify as "half" this and "half" that (or other fractions and delineations), the serpent's lie is defeated. We know we have been created whole and "very good."

This doesn't mean that if we *choose* to identify by percentages or as monoethnic, we're diminishing our wholeness.

There are benefits and drawbacks to both. Those of us who look ambiguously "in the middle" may find it easier to visit both camps but find ourselves kept at arm's distance in both. Those of us who look "fully" one ethnicity may choose to identify by one phenotype or the other. If we identify with our primary phenotype, we can gain community; but that may be at the expense of the other parts of our identity. If we identify against our phenotype, we may be accused of being fake; or we may be able to do good justice work.

None of these choices mean that we're denying who we are. The truth is, we mixed folk are not mere scientific "mixtures" that can be separated into constituent parts; we are scientific "solutions" (we'll look at the truth and implications of this silly pun next) who are whole and inseparable. And we have the right to identify our ethnic and cultural heritage as God leads us.

Mixed siblings, no matter how we identify, the important truth is that our blood is not striped, polka-dotted, or zig-zagged based on our differing ethnicities. The lie that a person's value is defined by percentages is just that: an evil lie from the pit of hell. Blood quantum, originally used by the government to oppress Native peoples and decrease tribe sizes, is a practice of placing emphasis on percentages. It came from privileged folks setting unbiblical boundaries and excluding others (much like the one-drop rule applied to African Americans) and has been used to restrict, dehumanize, and enslave people of color in a number of ways.

And it's still a complicated matter. Chickasaw scholar Elizabeth Rule says that she "uses the term 'Colonial Catch 22' to say that there is no clear answer, and that one way or another, people are hurt."[13] Whether in its original use or now (as it's practiced by sovereign tribal nations in the distribution of resources), blood quantum rules are a complicated part of Native identity, and especially so for mixed folks.

Regardless of how they're used today, the lie undergirding methods like blood quantum, the one-drop rule, and other percentage-based ways of determining ethnicity is that of "genetic purity," measuring a supposedly desirable whiteness against the other races, which are seen as a threat that can "pollute" that whiteness. Stu, in his Black and White identity, knows there is always the danger of affirming (even unintentionally) the false ideals of racial purity and White supremacy. Cass, thinking about his White and Native heritage, made this sobering statement: "Blood quantum is used to divide people in our tribe." Even in his sense of belonging, he realizes that others—who could and maybe should be included—are excluded.

Certainly it isn't true that "full" ethnicity or a specific skin tone is more desirable, nor do percentages make a person more valuable. Unfortunately, that lie is perpetuated, and sometimes by us mixed folks—even if only by our existence in the world. Majority-culture folks may find us more acceptable if we can "pass" for White. Or they may see us as a threat due to our lack of visible whiteness, whether from our ethnic heritage or our phenotype. Even in our efforts to reject the lies haunting our monoethnic minority siblings, we can sometimes go to the opposite extreme and lose the entirety of ourselves in the process.

No matter our ethnic story or appearance, we mixed folks carry within ourselves a clash between cultures. Whether it's across large racial boundaries (Black versus White, Asian versus Latinx, Native versus Middle Eastern, etc.) or within those categories (different Pan-African, Pan-Asian, Pan-European, Pan-American, or Indigenous countries and cultures, etc.), we carry the legacy of wars and of power differentials.

There's no doubt in my mind that in the United States especially, the Black Lives Matter movement is a necessary corrective to a society that constantly devalues brown skin. Full stop. Stemming from—not contradicting—that important truth is a subpoint: we people of multiethnicity (no matter our skin tone) should be treated like human beings, not objects. Our value is inherently from our Creator, and our right to loving community is the same as for anyone who can claim monoethnicity. We *can* push back against colorism, even while valuing the body God has given us. The embodied example of our multiethnic, Middle Eastern Savior teaches us how to do this.

IT'S DANGEROUS TO GO ALONE

You may find yourself especially weary in your multiethnicity, as you feel pressure to be a bridge between warring factions. This is a struggle for me too; my specific ethnic and cultural identity affects my worldview and my privilege. The entire point here is to remind all of us that humanity is not a monolith; folks with very similar backgrounds and experiences are unique unto themselves. I need to be reminded, as we all do, that my own experiences with stereotyping and cultural appropriation don't represent the whole.

Our varied stories are all the more reason why our voices are needed. As we multiethnic people know, when we feel disconnect with a general story, it's often due to others' limited experiences, not just our own. But when we receive each other's stories as a gift, we gain insight into others and ourselves. Because each of us has a unique set of circumstances, we're able to come alongside each other in solidarity. Together we can explore the implications of our right to define ourselves as we truly are. We can move beyond the stereotypes heaped upon us because of our appearance or upbringing, understand prototypes of our various cultures, and push forward in our identity in Christ.

Just like that awkward moment at a gathering when everyone happens to take a break in conversation at the same time and only one person is left talking, we mixed folks can feel like we're perpetual party crashers, an unwanted interruption to the regularly scheduled program. In our highly polarized, highly racialized society, we're often seen as an anomaly that creates discomfort.

But ultimately we can point to hope. We can be a humanizing presence in the midst of warring factions—but only in the strength God gives us and only in the community God gives us. We don't have to *be* a bridge to understanding, even as we strive to help build them and even though it may be true that mixed folks tend to be good mediators. We're often sought after as a "good middle ground," but sometimes we can just *be*.

Because we're bearing such a heavy load, we're also in need of care on all sides. Acknowledging this is important; as all weary minorities know, ignoring pain and systemic injustice doesn't make them go away. Just because our unhealthy human distinctions are social constructs doesn't mean they can be defeated with the wave of a magic wand—nor are we mixed folks mere objects like that metaphorical wand.

We aren't a mystical solution, though majority-culture folks may stereotype us as such. Sometimes the very existence of mixed folks is offered as a solution, as though, journalist Alexandros Orphanides humorously says, "A paradise of interracial and ethnically-ambiguous babies" will bring an unprecedented era of peace and harmony.[14] Although we're part of an increasingly global world, and even though more of us Kumbaya-crooning children are being born every day, society remains divided. We mixed folks are not magic talismans or a balm for our nations' wounds. Orphanides continues by stating that racism is not "passive—a vestigial reflex that will fade with the presence of interracial offspring, rather . . . [it is] an active system that can change with time."[15] We make the stands that God asks us to, but we trust in him to bring about the full kingdom in his own time. Even as we're willing to struggle and suffer for the Lord, we don't have to be martyrs who are sacrificed by others in this fight.

MULTIETHNIC PEOPLE OF COLOR

Our monoethnic *minority* siblings know the pain that can come from interactions with majority-culture people and their assumptions. But they often miss the pain that we may experience when interacting with monoethnic folks (minority and majority culture alike). Sometimes they buy into the stereotype that we mixed folks—especially those of us with White heritage—are all privileged people whose allegiance is to White normativity. This may or may not be true for some multiethnic people, but it can also be true of all people.

Our mixed ethnicity is not a guarantee of a solution, and it isn't inevitable that we prop up the systems in place. So when we ask our siblings of color to rethink their views of mixed folks, we're asking them to hear our stories and to seek to understand us better. If they truly want to love more and with greater insight, they'll make the effort. We can tell them, "Thank you for being willing to walk alongside us. We hope you know that we're committed to walk alongside you."

Mixed folks are often reduced to stereotypes—something to be stared at, analyzed, and consumed. In our in-betweenness, we're seen as a commentary on society, whether positive or negative. When monoethnic folks address us as human beings and not as *objets d'art*, we can find great joy in sharing our stories. We have the privilege of widening society's view of what ethnicity is.

Bekah, who identifies herself as a "White-passing" Middle Eastern and European American, enjoys learning about the prototypical Egyptian style of indirect communication. Through learning more about her culture, she's found a gracious alternative to the "What are you?" interrogation. She loves to ask others, "Would you tell me about your family?" When we give an invitation rather than an ultimatum, we can see each other both as representative of our ethnic backgrounds and as individuals.

PEACE BE WITH YOU, AND ALSO WITH YOU

Our purpose is never to pit one ethnic group against another or to try to prove how our experience as mixed people is the most difficult one. Yes, we mixed folks are often caught in the middle and either looked down upon or overlooked by all parties. But we aren't always the underdog, and we also mustn't be caught up by that stereotype. Even in the places where we aren't cared for, if we're following the way of Jesus, we rejoice in our struggles rather than wallow in our sorrows. We lament brokenness because we're seeking his kingdom—one where human hierarchies are completely upended as "the last will be first, and the first will be last" (Mt 20:16). Our goal is not to see who is better off or worse off, but rather to focus on him who is the best of all—though he suffered the worst punishment imaginable. Let us not be like Zebedee's sons, who wanted to be honored above all others. Instead let's strive to be made into the image of our humble Lord Jesus.

There is no perfect harmony this side of heaven, but we can work toward being a space of healing and connection as the Lord's embodied temple because he dwells in us (1 Cor 3:16-17; 2 Cor 6:16; Eph 2:18-22; 1 Pet 2:4-6). Not in spite of—but because of—how he designed us to be (in all our multiethnic identity), we can be that place within our very selves in union with Christ. Oh the joy when we see the people around us being all of who they are, all of who they're presenting themselves to be, and all of who God has created them to be!

In her ethnic journey, one of Bekah's moments of greatest joy was when her Arabic teacher told her, "I knew you were Egyptian from the first moment I saw you." Bekah said she almost cried, not just from being told that there *are* traces of her Middle Eastern heritage in her face, but also because her teacher didn't automatically assume she was only White. She felt very *seen* in that moment. Her teacher understood that Egyptian folks may look, dress, or speak a certain way, but she had room in her views for those who embody being Egyptian in a very different manner. And Bekah was willing to push into her Middle Eastern heritage and learn Arabic as an adult, which is difficult but rewarding work.

Karen, who also has White and Middle Eastern heritage, is excited to learn more about her Syrian family as well as her Greek, Scottish, and Irish ancestors. And she wants to be able to share what she's learning with others about Syrian culture. Though she also wasn't raised speaking Arabic, one of her greatest moments of joy was realizing that Syria is mentioned in Scripture. She said, "I get to look like Jesus! Some of the first Christians in Scripture looked like *me!*" This truth is no stereotype, nor is it simply a prototype. It's a scriptural and historical fact, one that speaks life to Karen. Embracing her place in the story means that she can delve into all of who she is.

Adichie concluded her TED Talk with this exhortation: "When we reject the single story, when we realize that there is never a single story about any place, we regain a kind of paradise."[16] When we mixed folks are seen (and see ourselves) as more than a stereotype or even a prototype, we can help create spaces of welcome and joy—sacred kingdom spaces in this liminal life. These shadows of the reality that is to come push back the lies from the multitude of demons who flail themselves against the gates of hell, eager to escape.

Praise God for Jesus' promise that his multiethnic church is stronger than anything that can slither past Hades' gates (Mt 16:18-19). Praise God for the complexity of his church universal, which we see reflected in the diverse array of his people's faces.

CHAPTER FOUR

Mixed Folks

Minorities of Minorities

Sometimes I forget there are freckles
on my face. It's the sort of thing where

I'm not always proud of my skin
for being light enough to illuminate the patches

of darkness that emerge from beneath it.
A colony of inconsistent color

spread out across this countenance. The remnants
of colonialism in this double-helix

of a body. When I was younger I was ashamed
of my mother for the heirloom

of her cheeks, always wondering why she
couldn't just keep them to herself.

CLINT SMITH III, "PASSED DOWN"[1]

"Daughter! You are Nepali! That is *all*," is a refrain that Binsa hears often. She is under a lot of pressure: to marry, to bear children, to "prove" her worth as a woman. Her Zimbabwean roots are something to be hidden; her family wants her to identify as solely South Asian and to emphasize her lighter skin.[2] This is a sadly common story for us multiethnic folks, as we try to fight against the dehumanizing evil of colorism while also celebrating ourselves in our entirety. We can often feel like a double minority that can't please either side.

The sociological study of intersectionality (looking at how different minority identities interact, overlap, and intensify each other) forms the basis for this *minorities of minorities* principle: because of the brokenness of the world, marginalized minority groups will have even further marginalized subgroups. While intersectionality usually is applied to the interactions between a person's race, gender, sexuality, and ability, etc., it can also apply across subsets of ethnicity. Even traditionally recognized minority groups in the United States (such as African Americans and Asian Americans) have those who are further on the margins (such as Black folks of Caribbean descent or those who have refugee narratives from a Southeast Asian country).

Minorities of minorities may actually identify very little with the larger minority group. The Caribbean experience of slavery and colonialism has marked differences from that of enslaved Africans in the continental United States. And this affects folks of Haitian descent in the United States as they consider the implications of how so-called "third world" Haiti is seen by our "first world" country. The Hmong story of displacement, migration, and integration into American society in some ways contrasts greatly with the experience of those in the previous waves of immigration from Central Asia.

There are many overlooked, underacknowledged groups: Native Americans (especially certain smaller tribes), South Asians, and the Indigenous peoples of Hawai'i, for example. Another group that occupies a distinct place within the larger minority experience is us mixed folks. Many generalizations are made about the overall ethnic minority experience in the United States; minorities of minorities often fall far outside of even those assumptions. Stereotypes concerning *monoethnic* minorities are damaging; for us multiethnic minorities, there can be specific pushback against us when we don't fit the stereotypes associated with any of our various ethnic backgrounds, or when we fit prototypes from more than one of our various backgrounds. Because monoethnic folks assume that ethnic traits are mutually exclusive across ethnicities, it can be difficult for those of us who are trying to live in more than one world at the same time.

For ethnic minorities in a majority-culture world, a life spent on the outside looking in can be exhausting. Recent studies have proven the long-term negative health effects of "*other*-ization" on minority groups—everything from increased suicide rates for Asian American students, as author Sarah Shin relates,[3] to drastically high maternal and infant mortality rates for Black women, as journalist Nina Martin reports.[4] In the midst of all this trauma and harm, one of the most healing experiences for any minority is to have time to rest and to be with people who are likeminded and can empathize through shared experiences. Spending time in a safe space where one is the norm—not the *other*—is an important part of healthy practices and rhythms. It can literally save our lives. But for many of us mixed folks, places where we are "normal" are few or even nonexistent.

SEEKING COMMUNITY

Community for mixed people can be difficult in many ways. Often we have to pick and choose from our ethnic backgrounds to have a connection with one part of our ethnicity, but at the expense of the other(s). Perhaps we can enjoy time with our Black friends and family, but that may require time away from our Latinx community. Or we may be able to develop deep relationships with other Asians but at the price of ignoring our European American roots.

Maria, who has Latino and White (Dutch Jewish) ancestry, relates that with her Latino friends she doesn't feel "Brown enough" because her identity is always questioned. With family, she's always treated as the *other*, being seen as "White to my Brown family and Brown to my White family." For her—and many of us—community requires constant self-guessing and feeling the need to justify ourselves.

Many of us mixed folks who have Native and European (or African) ancestry share the pain of not "looking Native enough" to overcome others' assumptions. Having Native family members seems to justify a claim to Native heritage, but there's the fear of coming across as appropriating and racist when exploring that heritage. Megan, who has Cherokee and Wendat roots (as well as Irish and Scottish) said she wishes "more Native people didn't assume I'm not Native because of how I look." Many of us agree with her desire to see an increased presence of "people who present White . . . [talking] about their ethnic backgrounds." But for those of us who don't fit stereotypes or prototypes, trying to share carries a risk. Megan finds great joy in being with other Native folks and learning about her heritage, but that is tempered with an uncertainty about whether she will initially be accepted or not, based on her appearance.

As we see with Binsa's story, even for those of us mixed folks without European ethnicity, colorism still comes into play. This is very much an issue for monoethnic minorities; it's only logical for it to be complicated for mixed people who have ancestors of any shade. In our resistance against injustice, we multiethnic folks have to bear the weight of these issues in the core of our being.

Even in the affirming, understanding company of other mixed folks, there can be a sense of loss. While we may be seen and celebrated in the entirety of our ethnicity as a mixed person, unless there are others with our exact multiethnic/ multicultural makeup, we are still alone. Even with other multiethnic folks, we often feel the need to modulate and adapt every cultural expression of who we are. We are the minorities of minorities, who are often left behind.

A REALITY CHECK

Please don't hear what I'm *not* saying. I'm not saying that a man with both Black and White ethnicity has it harder than a man who is "fully" Black. I'm absolutely not discounting that a multiethnic woman with lighter skin will experience privilege in a way that her darker-skinned sisters do not. But I am saying that the light-skinned multiethnic person will also experience marginalization—*in some areas*—where a darker-skinned, monoethnic person will not. Even for those of us mixed folks who don't have light-skinned, European heritage, we will most likely have some features and characteristics that are considered an anomaly in monoethnic circles—and that will affect us.

A large part of the minority experience in the United States is one of being *othered* due to White folks measuring us against the majority culture. We mixed people experience this in a certain way, even when with a group of monoethnic minorities, and we may feel crazy or guilty for our frustrations. Our experiences of *dis*privilege are not lessened by an experience of privilege in other areas. It isn't a math equation where the negative balances out the positive, or vice versa. But despite this truth, many monoethnic minorities will (understandably and even subconsciously) assume that our disparate experiences cancel each other out, and they will fail to see our legitimate hurts and needs.

The sad fact is that while colorism/racism is still a significant issue we must fight against, mixed folks are sometimes marginalized by siblings of color. Again, let me be perfectly clear. Because of the power dynamics inherent in racism, I don't believe that minorities can be "racist against" White folks. I'm not claiming that when "full" minorities are hurting or rejecting multiethnic folks that it's so-called "reverse racism." As author Jemar Tisby reminds us, that doesn't exist.[5] In terms of our racially unequal country, it isn't possible for an individual without inherent systemic privilege (due to the darkness of their skin) to be racist against another individual with high systemic privilege (due to the power inherent in their status as a lighter-skinned person). Prejudiced and angry, yes; racist, no. But I do believe that the harm against us mixed folks is real and that reconciliation in these cases should be part of the overall goal of affirming the value of the *imago Dei* in all humans. To be able to grieve and grow with us, monoethnic siblings must listen to our mixed stories of exclusion.

In a 2017 Code Switch podcast on National Public Radio, multiethnic cohost Shereen Marisol Meraji shared that she was called "off-brand" by her monoethnic minority friends.[6] While this was meant as a joke, it was devastatingly clever in the simplicity of its message: *You are not quite right. You're a cheap knockoff of a brand name—you may be able to pass from a distance, but upon closer inspection, it's clear that you don't make the grade. You are inferior.* Most of Meraji's friends probably don't mean to express that narrative when they affectionately tease her. But these moments speak nonetheless. For us mixed folks, many individual interactions with monoethnic people—in both minority and majority contexts—can add up to a sense of being "not quite right."

"PROBLEM" CHILDREN

In addition to awkward or hurtful experiences on an individual level, we mixed folks can face discrimination in many group settings and at many structural levels. Even in places where there is increased sensitivity to the needs of monoethnic minorities, there's often a structural ignorance about the needs and the value of mixed people. For example, I'm truly grateful that my ministry organization is often on the forefront of looking at holistic multiethnic ministry. In the

1940s, campus minister Jane Hollingsworth stood up in defense of racially integrated student work in New York City, even defying a board member to do so.[7] Whether it is through grassroots movements or at the highest levels, multiethnic and integrated ministry has long been one of our highest biblical values. But when it comes to meeting the needs of multiethnic minorities within minorities, we're definitely still learning.

When I joined my organization in 2006, multiethnic folks weren't as prominent as now, both in our movement and in the broader American culture. At my new-staff orientation, careful plans were made for several ethnic-specific breakout sessions discussing fundraising. Taking into account the prototypical experiences of minority ethnic folks, there were spaces for each minority group to discuss commonalities and needs. Black folks needed to be able to discuss the complexities of asking for support in the Black church. Asian Americans needed to be able to talk about fundraising and ministry in traditionally hierarchical spaces. Latinx staff needed a place to discuss how having a worldview centered on *la familia* ("the family") impacts Christian fellowship and finances.

And all of those staff needed to be able to discuss those cultural norms as a general rule, not as the exception to a majority-culture, individualistic worldview.[8] Even the White siblings needed a place to talk about their common experiences without feeling that they had to mince words or add caveats to avoid excluding minority siblings.

But there was a problem: me. As the emcee dismissed each group to their rooms for further discussion, I stood in the hallway, torn and embarrassed. *What about me? Where do I go?* echoed in my head as I wrestled with which group—and therefore which part of myself—to choose. Given my up-bringing, I was drawn to the Black staff, some of whom were already friends. But I decided (I still wrestle with the implica-tions of this choice, almost fifteen years later) that they needed a space where their dark skin wasn't in contrast to anybody's whiteness—a place where their skin tones were just the beautiful, normal reality.

I also knew that I would be fundraising mostly in majority-culture contexts, which suggested that I should stay with the White staff. But I suddenly felt, in a way I hadn't before, that to choose the majority-culture part of me *at that moment* would put me on a path to homogeneity once and for all. It felt like a larger choice was at stake. Perhaps it wasn't as dra-matic as it seemed at the time, but then and there—standing in the rapidly emptying hallway, watching doors shut behind folks who eagerly and confidently strode into each room full of their own people group—it was significant.

I might still be standing in that beige hallway if it weren't for a fellow mixed staff member who saw me awkwardly standing there. "Where do I go?" I asked plaintively, repeating the question that had been building up in me. In my physical, visible *otherness*, I was physically and visibly lost.

"Come with me, friend," Kylene said, leading me toward the Asian American session. "You do belong in here with us."

I went, but with trepidation. I had, at that time, never been to Thailand. I didn't speak the language nor did I really un-derstand the culture. I had no memory of my birth family, and much of my Asian features had faded since childhood. I neither looked nor felt Asian American. I had the very understandable fear that I would be met with confusion or even suspicion. I also worried that my presence would discomfit the Asian staff already there.

While the story has a mostly happy ending—I enjoyed my time and felt very welcomed—I left with a nagging sense that I didn't really fit in that group—that somehow I was an impostor.

DIVERSE PEOPLE, DIVERSE NEEDS, DIVERSE COMMUNITIES

So, what does this mean for those of us who are mixed minorities of minorities? We need and deserve greater community in three ways: with other mixed folks, with other believers, and most importantly, with Jesus. As we pursue holistic community, I believe firmly that we must first have our own spaces (in the same way that all minorities need safe spaces) where other people understand both the joy and the sorrow of being in multiple worlds. We need places where we can commiserate about displacement and the impostor syndrome, even as we celebrate our diversity and laugh about the awkwardness of code-switching. We deserve "tables" to sit at where we don't have to check constantly to make sure we haven't confused or offended folks who, by nature of their monoethnicity, have different shared experiences.

We need a place where we feel *seen* for who we are, which can be difficult. The nature of multiethnicity is often swallowed up by other cultures, and because of how phenotypes fit into the assumption that everyone is monoethnic, even we mixed folks may not realize when we meet other mixed folks.

A willingness to be vulnerable and share our stories can help with this. We need spaces where we aren't forced to choose one part of ourselves over another and where we can instead be authentic to the entirety of ourselves.

Many mixed folks feel like we're ghosts doomed to inhabit liminal spaces—otherworldly existences of neither here nor there. For some, we feel twice-invisible, overlooked in two or more cultural spaces, out of sync with the rest of the world and able to have only small interactions. Some of us feel doubly visible to a painful extreme, specters that haunt and disrupt monoethnic spaces. And many of us feel both—or neither—at one time or another.

We multiethnic minorities need to know that it's okay to be frustrated and grieved when we're excluded from mono-ethnic minority groups after being deemed, for example, "too White," "only Middle Eastern," or "not Black enough." We need to hear that our experience is real and significant. This can free us to inhabit our blended skin faithfully, while acknowledging the realities of our discriminated-against mono-ethnically Black and Brown siblings.

We all need to know that God delighted to make us just the way we are. We mixed folk deserve to hear, for example, that Creator can hold in tension what it means to be both Native and Hispanic. We have every right to be reminded that our Black and White heritage doesn't have to be in conflict. We need to tell ourselves and each other that our Latino and South Asian heritage is a valuable part of who we are, or that our Asian and Middle Eastern background is a unique blessing. It's so important for us multiethnic folks to hear these truths. Contrary to the lies that the evil one whispers in our ears, we are *not* cosmic mishaps. What joy when we can begin to believe that God designed us to be examples of the way that "in him all things hold together" (Col 1:15-20). What beauty we can see in ourselves when we realize that the Lord of all creation showcases his power in the way that he balances all the parts of us in perfect harmony.

Not only are we mixed folks unique witnesses to how Jesus holds all things together, we also are an echo of his new creation. As it specifically says in Colossians 1:17-18: "He is before all things, and in him all things hold together. And he is the head of the body, the church; he is the beginning and the firstborn from among the dead, so that in everything he might have the supremacy." We need to be reminded that—like Jesus!—we aren't a regrettable diluting of a supposedly pure bloodline. We need to know that we're a needed, intrinsic part of the church universal—and that we are not alone.

RECONCILING WITH MONOETHNIC SIBLINGS

Second in the type of growing community we deserve, we need ways to reconcile with our monoethnic siblings from both minority and majority cultures. If we have majority-culture ethnicity, we may need to repent of the ways we've ignored, hoarded, or despised our privilege. We also need to forgive those who have excluded or marginalized us. When we embrace our ultimate identity as "God's chosen ones, holy and dearly loved" of Colossians 3:12, we can pursue the cruciform forgiveness that follows in verse 13: "Forgive as the Lord forgave you." If we don't have any White background, we may need to repent of the ways we've judged other mixed siblings' privilege and experiences. We need to pursue unity both within and without.

I'm learning what it means to press into reconciliation with other Asian folks, even though I'm not fluent in indirect communication (in any ethnic or cultural setting). I need to be reminded that indirect communication doesn't mean ignoring or pulling away, though it may feel that way to me. I'm also learning that I'm absolutely "Asian enough," *and yet* it takes Spirit-empowered effort to better understand that part of me and my family. Culturally I have much to learn.

For some of us, there's a powerful joy in asserting our multiethnic heritage. Even as we acknowledge that saying we are "one-sixteenth Indigenous" or "one-fourth native Hawai'ian" can bring further pain to those who have been previously dehumanized by the false and harmful ideas of blood quantum and the one-drop rule, our mixed ancestry affects who we are. For others of us, we may find that our path to true flourishing lies in no longer doing the math on our ethnicity and instead in embracing all parts of ourselves, even if we identify as monoethnic. It can be powerfully formative for all people to learn more about their ancestors and heritage, and it's especially important for us mixed folks to be able to explore all of our different cultures without shame or judgment. Being able to receive feedback and instruction is intrinsic to everyone's process of learning more about identity; being weighed down with rejection, accusation, and disdain is not. This is especially true for those of us who are mixed.

In terms of my own journey, I'm also trying to remind myself constantly of the realities of discrimination against

Black and Brown people. I'm not ethnically Black, and it's vital that I not forget that. Despite identifying as culturally half Black and being raised in a mixed household, I have light-skinned privilege. Some may say that even though I wear my blackness "on my sleeve" when I wear one of my Black Lives Matter shirts, I don't wear it on my skin. I don't have the worldly lack of privilege (nor the rightful kingdom joy!) that comes with having much melanin. And although I'm ethnically Asian and White, I also have mixed-race cultural privilege due to my more subtle Asian features and, again, my light skin. I must not forget nor misrepresent this.

The more I read about Rachel Dolezal, who was active in the NAACP until she was exposed as White, the more I think that her lack of balance, her weariness from constant *othering*, and the ache of never quite fitting in was a large part of the problem. I wonder how different things may have been if she had just kept telling the full story of her ethnic and cultural heritage. Her background is similar to mine in some ways. She so identified with an African American pastor who "fathered" her and the church congregation that she was part of that she developed a deep heart for the *other*, for justice, and for Black culture. The issue became that she let people assume that she was ethnically part Black. She abridged the fullness of her story, probably because it was easier and less alienating for her. I can certainly understand the temptation.

On Facebook, I applied to two groups that focus on Black women and theology. For both, I told my whole story. One group admitted me with a reminder that it was primarily a safe space for Black women theologians, but others were welcome—a gift to those of us who are in that space as well as a risk to the primary audience. The other group sent me a kind "thank you for applying" message but fairly stated that their group was closed to non-Black folks. I was sad not to be included, but I understood. I shudder to think what may have happened if I hadn't told my whole ethnic/cultural story and had entered the group under false pretenses.

Reconciliation and deeper community were found not in being accepted into the Facebook group, but in the respectful, encouraging dialogue between me and the group moderators, both of whom affirmed me in my story and drew healthy boundaries for the good of others. In the case of the second group, my honesty was costly, but it was important not just for my own good and for the integrity and aims of the group, but also for the way in which it furthered discussion and helped us to see and care for the *other* a little better. I hope and pray that all of us are able to tell the entire truth about who we are, no matter the cost.

And yet, in contrast to all this, I also need to be authentic to myself, acknowledging and appreciating that I was indeed raised within prototypical Black culture and how much I identify with Black culture. When I was frustrated one day at work because I had been accused by a student of being "too angry," a Black colleague (commenting on my cultural up-bringing) said "Oh, you're not angry. You're just *passionate*. You're one of us!" Those words were very healing to me—as well as hilarious. Ky'sha, as a strong Black woman, was showing a willingness to see me in my cultural and ethnic entirety, which was a humbling gift.

FIGHTING THE GOOD FIGHT AND
SPEAKING TRUTH TO POWER

Siblings of multiethnicity and multiculturalism, it's important to remind ourselves, especially in issues of justice, that we do have a place on the frontlines: alongside—neither in front of nor behind—monoethnic people of color. We also need to remember that due to our unique perspective, we can be allies to other people of color in a very specific way. And lest we pass on (understandable but potentially harmful) frustration and backlash, we also need to rely on grace as we continue pursuing reconciliation with majority-culture siblings, some of whom may be just beginning the journey.

As I think about my mixed heritage and about reconciling with every part of myself, I also need to examine and appreciate the specific ways in which I am of European descent—and the implications of having light skin in a country that's intrinsically favorable to whiteness. Progress ebbs and flows. Perceptions of race have in some ways changed for the better, but more than that, people change. We multiethnic folks change. As it is for many mixed people, my ethnic journey looked very different in my teens than it does in my forties. As my appearance has changed, so have my experiences. As my understanding has grown, so has my teachability.

Leaning into my multiethnicity doesn't mean shaming myself for being White; it means pressing into what God is asking of me in the advantages and experiences he has given me. It means owning the ways in which I think, speak, and act in accord with majority-culture norms. It means embracing all of me, even when the White part of my heritage may play out as either bland or oppressive.

As we think about increasing community with monoethnic, majority-culture siblings, we have the right to both exhort and to encourage them. Let us tell them that as they press forward in learning to steward their privilege well, they must remember those of us who, regardless of our phenotype, are crying out "Where do I go?" We have every right to tell them, "Partner with those of us who do have some majority-culture privilege as we ask what healthy advocacy looks like, even as you acknowledge that we mixed folks do experience discrimination as well. Gospel-centric racial reconciliation stems from widening experience, not narrowing categories, and we mixed folks can teach much about shattering stereotypes, bridge building, and living in the gap." We don't have to let a majority-culture person (even one with non-ethnic minority status according to gender, sexuality, etc.) convince us that our multiethnicity means we don't count in these matters. We must rebuke that lie together.

We have the right and the privilege to tell White folks, "Remember that our minority status may mean that we're uniquely tired, uniquely alienated. We may not have the energy to show you the way very often." As with anyone in a minority position, it takes a lot of effort to be another person's perpetual interpreter, smoothing their way to understanding the minority experience. It can be exhausting to listen well and patiently as others grow, to hear their frustrations when they feel rejected by minority-culture siblings.

So we have not just the right but also the imperative to tell White folks, "Please, truly see us—both our gifts and our weariness. Love us well by listening. Remember our *constant feeling of otherness*, and make us feel welcome by getting to know us in all our complexity." We deserve to be heard, not only for our own good and for the edification of White folks, but for the flourishing of the church and the continued work of God's justice.

REALITY CHECK, PART TWO

As we think about the complications of pursing strong community with monoethnic *minorities*—those who identify with one minority group only—we mixed folks also have the right and the urgency to speak with both strength and humility. Honestly, this part of seeking community is the one I find the scariest, but also the most necessary. We must push in, as best we can, because Christ's love asks no less. Though it may be difficult for them to hear, we need to tell our siblings that we face discrimination of a specific type that they do not experience, while still acknowledging we do experience privilege denied to them by the majority.[9] These truths are not in competition. These realities do not require choosing sides; indeed, that is the beautiful message of our mixed reality.

We have the right to ask our fellow minorities, as Frazier puts it, to "please see us—both our wounds and our partnership. Love us well by acknowledging our place in the struggle. Remember that we occupy a difficult space among the marginalized, and affirm that we are family by acknowledging us in all of our intricacy."[10] So many of us mixed folks have stories of having no place that feels like "home" among the marginalized, even as we have stories of how we've experienced discrimination from being people of color. And we also have the pain of possibly being racist and discriminatory against our families and ourselves, of maybe hating our own bodies.

We not only can, but must, tell our monoethnic minority siblings, "Beloved, please let us weep and cry out to Jesus together. We aren't against each other in this fight for justice." We mixed folks are loved, seen, and charged with the gorgeous, terrifying blessing of communicating these truths. Many of our fellow minorities are ready to listen, having been moved by their own experiences and the Spirit's kindness.

A LEAGUE OF OUR OWN

My time with the Asian American small group at my new-staff orientation was an important part of my ethnic journey. It was important to me to choose to identify as Asian in that place and time. But part of the blessing of being mixed is the freedom to choose different spaces at different times. We mixed folks need places to explore different aspects of our multiethnicity. For example, I'm not an indirect communicator—a hallmark of much of Asian society. I proved it that day by finding someone in charge and firmly requesting that "multiethnic" be an option at the next ethnic-specific breakout. Apparently there were a few of us problematic people at the training, and so we pulled our five chairs into a tiny circle in the center of our windowless basement conference room, a little ark of people adrift in the middle of filigreed hotel carpet and towering stacks of ballroom chairs.

Ostensibly we met to talk about campus ministry and fundraising in light of our ethnic-specific context, but we mostly talked about our ethnic journeys and our experiences as minorities among minorities. It was a bittersweet time of affirmation for each of us—that we weren't alone in our ethnic loneliness; there were other outliers like us. None of us had answers to the conundrum of what to do with ourselves, both as individuals and as a group of mixed people within our larger organization. But none of us had answers *together*, which helped ease (though not completely address) our sense of disenfranchisement.

More than ten years later, I sat in the same hotel with the staff member (and now good friend) who had invited me into the Asian American small group. When I asked how the new-staff training went, she said that instead of five of us meeting awkwardly in the basement, there were almost twenty staff members there identifying as multiethnic. They met as part of the regular schedule—and on a main floor—and formed a cohort to encourage one another throughout their careers.

What a difference a decade can make! Yet change hadn't come without struggle and conflict. It came in part because monoethnic minority folks advocated for us—the minorities of minorities among them—by wielding some of their hard-won influence. It didn't come easily, as most callings don't.

Due to the systemic nature of discrimination, this progress also needed the partnership of majority-culture folks who were willing to advocate for us. Those monoethnic siblings—in many ways twice-removed from understanding multiethnic issues—had to yield much of their influence. They had to admit their lack of understanding about the minority experience in our organization. They had to work to understand and to advocate for change.

Change also required us mixed folks to step up and take a risk. We had to accept the possibility of being seen as pushy and ungrateful. We needed to rely on the intercession of the Holy Spirit in conflicts with both majority and minority monoethnic siblings. Ultimately change came because the Lord God was (and is) at work. I'm continually (and often painfully) reminded that as we push forward in faith, we must fully rely on the timing and the power of the Father, Son, and Holy Spirit, our triune God who shows us the perfect example of unity in diversity.

THE HEART OF TRUE COMMUNITY

Most crucial on the list of what mixed folks need and deserve is this: we must yearn for greater community with Jesus. This isn't a trite Sunday school answer; rather, it's the crux of our growth as mixed people. We must keep going back to Jesus and who he is, again and again. Matthew related in his Gospel that when the disciples were discussing Jesus and how the crowds identified him, Jesus asked them, "Who do you say I am?" (Mt 16:13-15).

Our identity must be derived from Jesus as we find our reality in who he is and what he has done for us. It's also important to understand that, as mixed folks, our identity comes as part of Jesus' mixed identity. This all requires having a clear answer to the Lord's question.

So who do we say he is? Peter proclaimed that Jesus is "the Messiah, the Son of the living God" (Mt 16:16). Through his sacrifice, he is our elder brother, who has enabled us also to be co-heirs of the new kingdom (Rom 8:17). Jesus is the one who has created all things and holds all things together (Col 1:16-17). When we look to the triune God to teach us what real community is, we can journey honestly with other mixed folks. When we bring all of ourselves into community with the Father, Son, and Holy Spirit, we can be alone in a room and not always hear the damning question "What are you?" reverberating in our heads. Instead we can hear who Jesus is and who we've become because of our union with him: part of his multiethnic family (Col 1:22).

This is what we'll explore next: what "identity in Christ" really means, and how the precious theological truths of healing and hope specifically apply to us mixed people. Identity in Christ is indeed the answer to our deepest longings for community. And as with all good theological discussions (ones that engage heart, soul, *and* mind), the answer is just the beginning of the conversation, not the end.

CHAPTER FIVE

Mixed Identity in the Multiethnic Christ

"OKAY, BUT WHY DO YOU HAVE to make it about race? Can't we just talk about the gospel? We're all children of God, and that's what matters, right?"

If there's one thing that gets Stu riled up (other than his favorite team's rival), it's what he calls the "child of God only" culture in the evangelical church. In that culture, an important theological concept—that we've been made heirs to the kingdom—is twisted into a way to ignore race, class, gender, and other issues of inequality. Especially for Stu, a mixed Black man, language and power dynamics matter. Brennan, with his Japanese and Chinese heritage, is also frustrated because when others "try to erase ethnicity and culture, . . . they communicate that being White is what brings unity."

We believers tend to misuse many phrases of the Christian faith, whether intentionally or accidentally. Well-meaning folks turn priceless biblical truths into meaningless clichés when applying them in a haphazard manner. For example, a family death receives a pat "Well, they're in a better place now," regardless of that person's faith background or the circumstances surrounding the passing. We weaponize complicated doc-trines by stripping them of their nuance: genuine struggles with mental illness are reduced to needing to "pray harder," as though the beautifully complex interactions of chemicals in our brains aren't a real or meaningful thing, as though the psalmist's cries aren't a prayer in and of themselves.

One phrase often used to diminish the distinctions and dignity of people of color is the hallowed phrase we just ex-plored: "identity in Christ." This mysterious, holy crux of our faith—that we're no longer in and by ourselves but instead have union with Christ, and thus with each other—is bas-tardized when used to force sameness and false unity in the body of Christ.

For us multiethnic people, "identity in Christ" can cause particular difficulties. Even when Jesus is accurately por-trayed as a nonwhite ethnic "minority" with dark skin, hair, and eyes, he is still perceived as being monoethnic, not mixed. So when we mixed folks are struggling with our various identities, especially as relating to our faith, Christ can all-too-often be held up falsely as a paragon of monoethnic wholeness and unity for us to emulate. The issue is not that we shouldn't base our identity in Christ and in his wholeness, because we should embrace all of our blessed reality and new status in Christ. The issue is the potential shallowness of that picture. A one-dimensional view of Jesus leaves us with a one-dimensional view of ourselves.

A MULTIDIMENSIONAL SAVIOR

In terms of both ethnicity and culture, Jesus was mixed. He chose to come to earth at the intersection of many different

realities. The more commonly touted ones are his one-person/
two-natures being, his coming first for Israel then for the
Gentiles, and his role as both priest and sacrifice. But God also
chose non-Jewish foremothers as part of the Messiah's heritage, and thus as part of his human identity. Matthew very
intentionally included Rahab and Tamar the Canaanites, Ruth
the Moabite, and Bathsheba (Uriah the Hittite's wife) in the
list of Jesus' forebears. Despite the large amount of faithful
scholarship on the person and identity of Christ, his mixed
identity is still largely unappreciated. Mention his multiethnic
lineage, and monoethnic folks are likely to doubt and to dis-
agree with you. When confronted with their faulty assumptions, people often argue with the clearly biblical fact of Jesus'
"muddy" ethnicity; they find it confusing and even threatening.

Some would say that it's already confusing enough to try
to comprehend his divine/human nature, but at least that's a
necessary aspect of understanding salvation in Christ as our
ultimate substitute (Mt 8:17; 1 Pet 2:24). They would claim
that the other mysteries we see in Christ are less important.
Right? Wrong. Many Christians rightly believe that Jesus is
the exemplary specimen of humanity, but find the idea of him
having a mixed identity problematic. How, they reason, could
a fragmented Jesus heal a fragmented world? Wouldn't he
need to be whole, unblemished,[1] and clear-cut? No, the fact
is that the covenant God didn't require sacrifices to be pale,
he required them to be *whole*. But when we assert that Jesus
is multiethnic, folks may be alarmed because of the "tragic
mulatto" trope which implies internal torment.

Some may ask, "Haven't we been exploring the tragedy of
being multiethnic?"

Well, yes and no. It's true that we mixed people may find ourselves conflicted and uncertain. Hopefully our mono-ethnic allies can resonate with a feeling of in-betweenness due to some other demographic characteristic, such as socio-economic status, sexual orientation, or cultural and personality traits. Conversely some of us multiethnic and multicultural folks have little to no internal disconnect. That is certainly not a bad thing, beloveds. Perhaps you feel that you fit in just fine, and this all seems a bit odd.

Lack of internal disconnect is actually the goal, something to be worked out over a lifetime of following Jesus. The essence of being mixed is not wallowing in a supposed lack of symmetry, but rather inhabiting the reality of our liminal existence; we might not fit neatly into established norms. The difference lies in how we experience ourselves and others, in how we find wholeness in our interactions—both external and internal.

As a mixed person, Jesus experienced—he *embodied*—wholeness, even as he wrestled with understanding himself and the Father's will for him. The problem isn't in being mixed; the problem is in multiethnicity being seen as incomplete, abnormal, and undesirable.

THE PERFECT OFFERING FOR IMPERFECT PEOPLE

Jesus could have chosen a "pure" Jewish ethnicity, but he very purposely ordained for himself a multiethnic lineage. Why? And how do we see that in relation to the writer of Hebrews' proclamation that Jesus "through the eternal Spirit offered himself unblemished to God" (Heb 9:14)? When Paul makes a distinction between the life of the

flesh and the life of the spirit in Romans 8:9, the implication is not that a faithful Christian life is one devoid of
the reality of our lived-in bodies. Rather, "if Christ is in
you, then even though your body is subject to death because of sin, the Spirit gives life because of righteousness.
And if the Spirit of him who raised Jesus from the dead is
living in you, he who raised Christ from the dead will also
give life to your mortal bodies because of his Spirit who
lives in you" (Rom 8:10-11).

Three things to note from this passage: (1) our bodies are
subject to death because of sin—not because of ethnicity,
(2) the Spirit gives life to Jesus—and through him, us—
because of Christ's righteousness, and (3) the joys and
promises of life in our bodies are not limited to our future
glorified bodies, though that's the main point of the passage.
But somehow, mysteriously and miraculously, our mortal
bodies are the seeds of what our glorified bodies will be. As
the Spirit indwells, so he brings new life. Christ was the unblemished and perfect sacrifice because the internal reality of
his trinitarian union with the Holy Spirit affected the righteousness of his entire being, and not just spiritually.

When we look at relevant passages in Ephesians 2, we
see that God has created a new humanity, a new type of
being. For this new race, Jesus' reconciliation supersedes
human ethnicity, but it *also* undergirds and highlights it.
Christ didn't nullify the inherent diversity in our bodies;
rather, he destroyed the "barrier, the dividing wall of hostility" between Gentile and Jew (Eph 2:14). It was oblit-
erated in the sacrifice and person of Christ, explains
theologian Clinton E. Arnold in his exegesis of chapter two.

For he himself is our peace, who has made the two groups one and has destroyed the barrier, the dividing wall of hostility, by setting aside in his flesh the law with its commands and regulations. His purpose was to create in himself one new humanity out of the two, thus making peace, and in one body to reconcile both of them to God through the cross, by which he put to death their hostility. He came and preached peace to you who were far away and peace to those who were near. For through him we both have access to the Father by one Spirit.

Consequently, you are no longer foreigners and strangers, but fellow citizens with God's people and also members of his household, built on the foundation of the apostles and prophets, with Christ Jesus himself as the chief cornerstone. In him the whole building is joined together and rises to become a holy temple in the Lord. And in him you too are being built together to become a dwelling in which God lives by his Spirit. (Eph 2:14-22)

Once believers are "in Christ" (εν Χριστω), as Paul emphasizes multiple times throughout Ephesians, we're able to be in community with God and thus with other humans,[2] who retain their distinctive ethnic identities. Because our ultimate identity is in Christ, we're able to have a peace on which to build other aspects of our identity, both as individuals and corporately.

Let's look at the reason we're being built together. Paul writes of the mystery that when we are in Christ, he is in us, even as he and the Father are one: "And in him [Christ Jesus] you too are being built together to become a dwelling in which God lives by his Spirit" (Eph 2:22).

The deep reality of this never fails to amaze me. Too often, in the rush and busyness of life, the mention of it might not immediately faze me. But when I stop and think on the reality of being in Christ—the astounding, mysterious truth of being one with God—it leaves me speechless. The risen Lord Christ, in all his inexplicable complexity, beauty, and power, chooses fallen, mismatched, fragmented people to build his dwelling place, his *home*. This leaves me breathless, and it leaves me hopeful.

Just as Jesus still bears the wounds of his crucifixion even after his resurrection, he is multiethnic for all eternity. This is not coincidental nor irrelevant; it's part of his glorious redemption purpose. That's the reality that helps me to find wholeness, no matter what part of my ethnic identity I am (or am not) pushing into. Jesus is the firstfruits of all the redeemed heirs of the promise (1 Cor 15:23), and we are being constructed in his likeness.

The more we think about it, the more unthinkable it becomes. Our primary identity in Christ makes all other identities possible.

In terms of our relationship to the three persons of the one God, while we are *one with* the Father and the Holy Spirit is *in us*, we are *in Christ*. He is the new humanity, and we find our identity, our meaning, and our beauty in him. But as we explored earlier, the phrase "your identity is in Christ" is often hurled at those of us on the margins, those who don't fit into majority-culture norms.

REBEL WITH A CAUSE

When we look at the person of Christ, we see that he is and was a man who was far from conforming to an established cultural paradigm. In addition to his multiethnicity, he was born into and lived in poverty (Mt 2:6; 8:20; Phil 2:7), was called unclean and blasphemous by the religious authorities of the day (Jn 10:20, 33), and showed compassion to outcasts such as the demon-possessed (Mt 8:16), religious sect members and women (Jn 4:9), and those in desperate need of physical healing (Mk 5:29; Lk 5:24). Contrary to the lies we've been led to believe, Jesus, in the fullness of his humanity, isn't a one-note personality. He isn't easily boxed into expectations, because he does his Father's will, not the will of the world.

If we're honest, none of us is a flat personality. All people have layers of complexity, though self-preservation may require hiding some of them. But as we cast off our old person—the one deadened and tripped up by sin—and step into our new identity in Christ, we must be very careful to understand what that does and doesn't mean—not just theologically but also practically.

HEADS UP! "IDENTITY IN CHRIST" INCOMING

Being in Christ doesn't mean losing our humanity and distinctiveness; it means reclaiming it. Christ was the earthly embodiment of the wholeness of the fruit of the Spirit (Gal 5:22-23), fulfiller of both the letter and the spirit of the law. In him we see the miraculously held tension between being a unique individual and being a member of a community. We see how he is both just and merciful—calling out the

Pharisees' lack of faith as well as highlighting the saving faith of people such as the bleeding woman. Exploring her Latina identity in the book *Hermanas: Deepening Our Identity and Growing Our Influence*, one of the authors, Noemi Vega Quiñones, reminds us that "it was the bleeding woman's *faith* that was praised by the Gospel authors—it was her courageous action to step forward and just touch his cloak!"[3]

And when Jesus named her "Daughter," he didn't require her to stop being who she was; he showed her that her true identity was in relation to him. Being in Christ didn't mean she was suddenly another race, gender, or personality. It meant she was recognized as belonging to the family of God, which gave healing and joy to all aspects of her human identity. "Just like the bleeding woman, we find our name and our true identity in Jesus. We are mijas [daughters] and hermanas [sisters] in the kingdom of God!"[4] And if we are *mijas* or *mijos* ("sons"), we are—in a nongendered term—truly God's children.

All three authors of *Hermanas* relate to the mestiza experience and what that means for their identity as beloved *mijas*. As she grows in confidence in her identity in Christ and his care for her, author Natalia Kohn Rivera is learning how to answer the perpetual question "What are you?" that she gets due to her mixed-race phenotype. As she grew older, she says, her answer "began to come from my heart," going from "rolling my eyes at my biracial complexities to smiling with confidence stating that I am both Argentinian and Armenian."[5]

Author Kristy Garza Robinson shares that she has spent her life "geographically and emotionally straddling the border of the United States and Mexico, finding my home and feeling displaced in both countries and cultures."[6] Vega Quiñones also had a "multifaceted childhood," growing up speaking a different language to each of her parents and, having immigrated to the United States, living in the intersection between poverty and wealth.[7]

These women have different identity stories, and although only one fits the multiethnic category as defined previously, all of these *hermanas* understand the importance of a true, multifaceted identity in Christ. In discussing the multicultural biblical heroine Esther, Garza Robinson issues an invitation to us: "Take up your identity just like Esther, wherever you are on your ethnic identity journey. . . . [Believe that] God created you with intention and purpose in all things." She exhorts those of us who have "embraced your identity, knowing it to be a gift of God. . . .Offer this part of your identity to the Lord's work in and around you."[8]

The multiethnic story is never one of either/or, even when we choose to focus on one aspect of our identity over another. The beauty and mystery of Christ's identity is that he can strengthen and undergird this reality in us. Our mixed identity is a gift to be offered back to him in service, as we are one with him and partnering with him to speak the good news of hope and healing.

Human identity is a precarious thing. Human labels, including ethnicity, author Michael Card writes, can't fully answer

the basic question of who I am. What inevitably must happen, if I hope to be able to answer the ultimate question, is that all these incomplete identities must be stripped away in what is most often a painful process. Only after we arrive at the end of our incomplete and false identities are we ready to receive the final and conclusive answer to the question of who we really are.[9]

For us mixed people, however, a key part of this "painful process" is inherent to who we are. Our ethnic identities—however "incomplete and false" they may be—are challenged from all sides, seemingly from birth. We know that, as Card says, "perhaps the most fundamental human question is, 'Who am I?' Our peace rests in finding the answer to this question. The greatest moments of emotional stress and upheaval occur when our self-understanding is challenged or violated, when we don't know who we are."[10] This is a reality that many mixed folks already know how to inhabit. We're already well aware that ethnic identity can be fickle and therefore not something to count on for our ultimate identity.

So, what is the identity of a Christian? As Card continues, the answer comes straight from Jesus:

> The Beatitudes of Matthew 5 will forever redefine the identities of the followers of Jesus; they are the poor, mourning, gentle, hungry, merciful peacemaking ones who, above all, are persecuted. According to this radical new identity, they will possess the new kingdom of which Jesus is the king. The unclean leper, the bleeding woman, the blind and the lame will all discover a new healed identity in Jesus.[11]

SPIRITUAL ETHNICITY IN A LINEAGE OF FAITH

It's not that we must be ethnically similar to Jesus, as though we mixed folks have an advantage over monoethnic siblings. But when we're *spiritually* similar to Jesus, we can find our identity in him and bring meaning and fullness to our multiethnic identity. Being mixed is just one of the many ways we can identify with Christ in his body, but it's a valuable one that's often overlooked or even dismissed. As our eyes are opened to the experiences of our siblings around the globe, there's something uniquely beautiful in talking to image bearers who *do* look like the historical and resurrected Christ. Karen, in her Middle Eastern and White ethnicity, delights in the fact that "I get to look like Jesus!" and in the knowledge that "some of the first Christians in Scripture looked like *me*." As she reads the stories of early believers walking the sands of the Middle East, she realizes that she's no mere abstraction of what unity in Christ looks like. She is a walking, talking, Spirit-filled, *and embodied* example of the work of reconciliation Christ has done within himself and between God and man.

So being "in Christ" is no mere phrase, no lackluster truism. Being in Christ is everything, and it's tied up in our embodied ethnicities and cultural realities. This isn't exclusive to those of us who are multiethnic, but as with everything else, there's a unique beauty in how we mixed folks are made in the image of God and how we can see a distorted image redeemed. All believers have their "spiritual ethnicity" in Christ; we are heirs of the promise and Abraham's children by faith in the work of the Messiah, not through human lineage. But we multiethnic folk can also have the unique joy of knowing that our mixed spiritual lineage is reflected in our mixed bodies. We are a part of that sign and seal of the embodied glory that is to come.

In the same way that creatures are made in God's image but are not him, our redeemed selves are being made into Christ's image but are not him. He is the elder sibling, we the younger children who still inherit the riches of the kingdom by his generosity and mercy. Being made into the image of Christ doesn't mean we look like gods; it means we showcase the reality of our creator God as he intended us to, in our human bodies. And contrary to Gnosticism, which would tell us that our bodies are irrelevant, our beautiful diversity is mysteriously and unfathomably reflective of our God. Tisby reminds us that, contrary to colorism, which would tell us that we all must be one pale shade, our skin tones—dark and light—reflect the spectrum of beauty that God has created.[12]

There's a wholly unique and beautiful way in how we mixed folks can see—and thus help to build—the "here and not yet" kingdom. Multiethnic folks with a strong sense of identity can be agents of the peace that we have in Christ. Timothy knew this well. When Paul mentioned Timothy's mixed heritage in 2 Timothy 1, he was very intentional to mention Timothy's foremothers who were pillars of the faith. Paul recalled Timothy's "sincere faith, which first lived in your grandmother Lois and in your mother Eunice" as a testament to God's goodness in continuing a Christian lineage in Timothy's multiethnic family (2 Tim 1:5).

With his "Greek father and Jesus-following Israelite mother," as theologian Christopher A. Porter puts it (referencing Acts 16:1[13]), Timothy knew what it was like to live in different worlds. It's interesting to note that he was uncircumcised until Paul decided that it would help the ministry among the Jews (Acts 16:3), and that in 2 Timothy, Paul reminded Timothy that Jesus was descended from David (2 Tim 2:8).

Clearly Timothy's Jewish and Greek heritage didn't negate his identity in Christ. Instead, it increased his ability to minister in a variety of places. His unique upbringing in a multiethnic and multicultural family shaped his time as the first bishop of Ephesus, overseeing a church that was mostly non-Gentile. But Timothy would have also related to Paul's exhortation to the Gentile church members to remember that "formerly you who are Gentiles by birth and called 'uncircumcised'... were separate from Christ... but now in Christ Jesus you who once were far away have been brought near by the blood of Christ" (Eph 2:11-13). Because of his mixed identity, Timothy could minister as both a Jew and a Gentile to Jews and Gentiles alike.

Moses was also someone who knew what it meant to be in different worlds. Bible study author Neil Rendall relates that

> Moses was not simply an Israelite who just happened to have spent the first forty years of his life in the Egyptian halls of power ... [nor was he simply] a refugee in the land of Midian. .... [Moses was a] combination of all that he had lived through. He was an Egyptian-Midianite-Hebrew tri-cultural man who cannot be separated and forced into only one part of his identity.[14]

Moses' years of growing up in Egypt and then his exile in Midian prepared him for the work of setting God's people (Moses' people!) free. When Moses met the LORD in the desert, he asked "a good question, . . . an identity question, 'Who am I?'"[15] Many times we mixed folks have asked this question. So many times we've cried out the Lord, wondering if there's a good answer.

Moses' answer—and thus ours—is that "unknown to Moses, God had used these years [of being in various cultures and places] to make him into a tri-cultural man who would never be all that God meant him to be until he fully accepted his unique Egyptian-Midianite-Hebrew identity." Moses needed to accept his multiethnicity/multiculturalism, not as his final identity, but as an identity that pointed him back to the Lord. And Rendall further encourages us when he says, "The life of Moses is a great affirmation for [mixed folks]. They have unique gifts that God can use for a world that contains a growing multitude of refugees. . . . God uses all of who we are, not just part of our identity."[16]

SPIRITUAL ETHNICITY IN A LINEAGE
OF FAITHFUL MOTHERS

Timothy's mother and grandmother, Lois and Eunice, aren't listed in Jesus' lineage, for obvious reasons. But there are five women who were included in Jesus' Matthew 1 genealogy: Tamar, Bathsheba, Rahab, and Ruth, as well as his mother Mary. Though apparently monoethnic and mostly non-Jewish, they all understood multiethnic and multicultural power dynamics, and they mothered mixed children. They're an important part of Jesus' multiethnic lineage, and thus an important part of ours.

Tamar, mother of Perez (by Judah) was from the land of Canaan, and understood the importance of securing heirs for her deceased husband and for holding her in-laws accountable. As Bathsheba's husband was a Hittite, it's reasonable to assume that she was too, especially since Matthew lists her as one who "had been Uriah's wife" (Mt 1:6). Despite David's sin against her and Uriah, and the subsequent death of their first child, God chose this multicultural, non-Jewish woman to bear the mighty King Solomon, and to further the line of kings building toward Jesus.

Rahab (like Ruth would later) proclaimed the covenant Lord God to be her own. Though she rejected her identity as a Canaanite citizen of Jericho who worshiped other gods, she no doubt maintained at least some of her cultural mindsets and practices. Even before she was grafted into the Israelite nation, her willingness to cross cultures and see the *other* is evident. It's her faith, obedience, and her welcome to the Hebrew spies that is praised in Hebrews 11:31. These values were no doubt passed on to Boaz, who had mercy for the "poor and the foreigner" (those whom God provided for in his laws regarding gleaning [Lev 19:9-10]). Boaz's multiethnic heritage wasn't a threat to his rightful worship of the Lord, it was an inherent part of how he lived out universal truths in his specific time, place, and culture.

Ruth the Moabite was willing to follow her mother-in-law Naomi because she'd experienced the love of the covenant God in her crosscultural marriage to a Hebrew. Naomi's faith—even in the face of great sorrow and adversity—was a testimony to God's goodness. God carefully designed this multiethnic lineage for Jesus, and this is an encouragement to us mixed folks! Their entire family—Naomi, Ruth, Boaz, Obed their son (and on down the line)—wasn't less

authentically part of God's people because it was multiethnic/
multicultural. No, it was proof of God's love for the nations
and a promise of the Messiah to come!

Professor and commentary author Kathryn Lois Sullivan
delighted in showing how the inclusion of Rahab and Ruth
in Jesus' genealogy was "offending [to] racial purists" as she
skillfully exegeted her way through the Bible to refute "op-
ponents of interracial justice." In looking at the story of
Rahab, Ruth, and others, Sullivan showed that "there is no
divine sanction for the superiority of one race, or for racial
segregation, or against interracial marriage."[17] God has tes-
tified to the goodness of all ethnicities—and therefore *our*
mixed ethnicities—throughout the Bible and in the person
of Jesus.

So the question remains: How do we follow the example of
these mighty witnesses and faithfully live into our fullness of
being *in* Christ? Rather than offering "identity in Christ" as yet
another identity to wrestle with and bear up under, let's look at
specific ways to *rest* in our Christlike identity and to move
forward in understanding the unique ethnicity that God's
given us. Though we struggle, being mixed really is a blessing.

CHAPTER SIX

Exploring and Nurturing Mixed Identity

So God breathed life into Adam and Eve.
When they opened their eyes, the first thing they ever
saw was God's face. And when God saw them he was
like a new dad. "You look like me," he said. "You're
the most beautiful thing I've ever made!"
God loved them with all of his heart. And
they were lovely because he loved them.

SALLY LLOYD-JONES, *THE JESUS STORYBOOK BIBLE*

WE'VE AFFIRMED THE GOODNESS OF GOD in making mixed people, and we've contextualized the rooting of our identity in Christ. Now we have to ask, "How does this affect each of us in our daily walk with Jesus?" We've also painted a hopeful picture of multiethnic folks thriving, not merely surviving, in the wholeness of their shifting identity. This may lead us to wonder, *What can we do to foster this growth in ourselves?* While there are many mixed heroes of the faith, there has been little scholarship on forming a mixed identity and far too few resources giving a practical roadmap for what a multiethnic identity journey could look like. But there are a few.

As we've studied folks like Moses, Ruth, and Timothy, we've seen how their mixed ethnic and cultural stories informed their lives. Resources like Dr. Maria P. P. Root's *Bill of Rights for People of Mixed Heritage* (1993) and Sundee Tucker Frazier's book *Check All That Apply* provide frameworks to think about multiethnicity in a larger context. Unfortunately, current methods for exploring identity in Christ tend to either ignore ethnicity (and thus whitewash it) or just focus on the monoethnic experience (and often in relation to whiteness). But we mixed folks do have stories to tell, wisdom to share, and joy to foster. Stemming from the ways in which all believers are embodied testaments to the gospel, we multiethnic people can showcase the joys and the sorrows of mixed-identity growth in our everyday lives.

FOR EVERYTHING THERE IS A SEASON

Kylene feels a lot of joy in her Shanghainese and White heritage, and she loves walking with other mixed folks in their identity formation. She enjoys hearing their stories and says, "No two people have shared the same experience, but there are commonalities that resonate with mixed people. . . . One day you can be walking along feeling totally content in all of your mixedness, and the next day/minute you feel like hiding."

As with every human endeavor, working out identity is a lifelong process, and we mixed folks feel this deeply. Kylene shares that in this "never-ending journey as a mixed [ethnicity] Christian, I truly believe I will never feel like a whole person until I get to heaven." This isn't a bad thing—this feeling that something is missing—but it does take working through, especially if we want to help others tell their stories.

The Christian walk is a series of triumphs and failures, of contentment and shame. Even as we are being perfected into the image of Christ, our earthly progress comes in fits and starts. We learn to see others through Jesus' eyes, and then we cycle back to selfishness. We study a passage in the Bible on kindness, and then we promptly forget everything when our patience is tested. This is the nature of our "here and not yet" status.

THE MULTIETHNIC IDENTITY DISCIPLESHIP CYCLE

To harness the up-and-down nature of life, my organization has a "discipleship cycle" for engaging the Bible and making disciples (see Mt 28:19).[1] It has been adapted into various systems and activities throughout our ministry, so here I've adapted it into a model for exploring and nurturing our mixed identity day by day, as well as over a lifetime.

The basic InterVarsity discipleship cycle has three sections: "Hear the Word," "Respond Actively," and "Debrief and Interpret." Applying this to our mixed-identity development yields three parts:

1. Pray About Ethnic Formation

2. Explore Ethnic Identity

3. Apply Truths to the Christian Walk

Each of these three parts has specific steps within it. But first, let's first look at the Multiethnic Identity Discipleship Cycle as a whole.

ECHOING THE ALPHA AND THE OMEGA,
THE BEGINNING AND THE END

One of the things I love about a three-part cycle is the way it mirrors the Trinity. First, we ask God the Father to hear our prayers for wholeness and insight from a place of stillness and need. Next we ask the Holy Spirit to guide us as we actively respond to the truths we see in Scripture, so we can learn and grow. Then we review what God has shown us in how he created us good and redeemed us in Christ. Last (but not really), we start the cycle over again, hopefully with some measure of increased insight and trust.

This rhythm allows us to focus on our mixed identity without losing sight of God. We start by kneeling at God's throne. Even as we move about and do the necessary work of learning and growing, we do so from a place of utter dependence on the Lord. And when we circle back to locating ourselves in Christ, we remember that his sacrifice is what allows us to "approach God's throne of grace with confidence" (Heb 4:16).

Someday Jesus will come back, and our mixed selves will join the multiethnic body in worshiping him forever. Until then, we are continually reminding ourselves "he must increase, but [we] must decrease" (Jn 3:30 ESV). This doesn't mean we forget ourselves entirely; why would we when God never forgets or abandons us? It does mean that we submit ourselves to the Lord and reflect his glory back to him. We grow as disciples of Jesus by continually locating ourselves in him.

As with any human model, the Multiethnic Identity Discipleship Cycle isn't perfect, but it can foster the work of preparing us for the new heavens and the new earth. As we learn to depend on God more, we are fulfilling the Great Commission: to make disciples of all the earth, which includes us. Whether we're doing the work by ourselves or in community, we look more like Jesus when we're submitting to the Father's will and understanding our need of him. Because "we are God's handiwork," understanding our multiethnicity is part of the "good works, which God prepared in advance for us to do" (Eph 2:10).

PART ONE OF THE MULTIETHNIC IDENTITY DISCIPLESHIP CYCLE: PRAY ABOUT ETHNIC FORMATION

In pursuit of a wholeness and unity that only comes from and with Jesus, our first step must always be prayer. When we seek him first, he'll then bless us with other important gifts (Mt 6:33). A journey into better understanding our ethnicity must start with humility and listening, *before* we do the important work of interpretation, exploration, and application. So we go to the first part of the cycle.

We come vulnerably to the God of the universe and ask him to see us, hear our prayers, and speak to us in kindness. We seek to be reminded of truth as well as to be able to gain new understanding about who he is and how that affects us. We bring our concerns and questions about what it means to be multiethnic like Jesus is. This part of the cycle is very personal and in many ways requires us to be still before the Lord, so each of us will approach this differently. My advice is to enter into prayer with a specific request to help ground our wandering, doubtful minds. As spiritual mentor Ruth Haley

Barton wrote in *Invitation to Solitude and Silence*, "Sacred space is a *physical place . . . a place set in time* [and also] *a space in our soul* that is set apart for God and God alone. . . . As you enter into your time of silence . . . ask for a simple prayer that expresses the openness and desire for God that you have been experiencing."[2]

Breathing out a prayer such as "Teach me who I am, Lord" can help us to remember that we are children of God. We depend on our identity in Christ and at the same time seek to understand the beauty of our mixed identity. Asking "Jesus, let me look like you" can remind us of his embodied multi-ethnicity—his beauty inside and out. Crying out "Holy Spirit, I feel lost; please groan with and intercede for me" can be a prelude to great comfort even in sorrow, when there seem to be no answers.

This time of prayer can be part of an extended retreat, a personal quiet time, or even a group exercise with space for individual processing. Or it can simply be a repeated prayer before, during, or after wrestling with our mixed identity—a quick reminder that we aren't alone. God is with us in our awkward interactions with others, moments of impostor syndrome, and our painful sense of having no home.

PART TWO OF THE MULTIETHNIC IDENTITY DISCIPLESHIP CYCLE: EXPLORE OUR ETHNIC IDENTITY

Once we've centered ourselves in God (hardly a one-time thing!), we can explore our ethnic identity further. Here we do the practical work of learning on our own and with others. This is where we ask about our family members, research our ancestors, read books about our cultures. In this part of the cycle, we're actively responding to what God is doing through the resources he has given us. We may choose to do this from a variety of perspectives. Some days, we may feel an affinity for a specific part of our ethnicity, while on other days, we may lean toward the totality of being mixed as our primary identity. On one day, we may want to focus on something other than our multiethnicity, and other times, we may want to explore how the various parts of our mixed identity interact with each other.

Because mixed identity can be so fluid, figuring out what parts of ourselves to learn about can be difficult. Jennifer Hollingsworth, who is Filipina and White, has developed the Four Postures model for better understanding how we perceive ourselves and the world around us.[3] Having honed this model through various seminars, speaking engagements, and small-group studies, Jen has graciously offered it as a sort of "walking stick" on our multiethnic journey. The model doesn't propose a right/wrong dichotomy or even a linear model of progress. Instead, it's a flexible group of varying postures that we can take toward our ethnic identity, a spectrum of places we may find ourselves in.

Jen makes it clear that the model is not a rigid construct, but "a tool to help move the conversation forward. It is an abstraction of life. I recognize the irony of creating categories to describe something that is an attempt to deconstruct those of us who defy categories . . . [but] each posture has potential to be redemptive . . . none is inherently better than the other." There isn't a linear way in which a mixed person "should" move through the Four Postures model; rather, using this framework can help us identify where we've found ourselves at any given time.

I've summed up the four postures as *solidarity identity, shifting identity, substitute identity,* and *singular identity.* We mixed folks have the freedom to move fluidly between the four postures as often as is best for us, and we shouldn't fear judgment or reprisal. In many instances, we may move between the four postures without even realizing it. Let's look at each posture one by one.

Posture 1: solidarity identity. When in this posture, we align ourselves with a monocultural experience, perhaps in both behavior and appearance. Some of us mixed folks might choose (or find ourselves in) this solidarity-identity posture in varying circumstances. Others of us may inhabit this posture for a longer period of time (or even a lifetime). Our phenotypical appearance (and how that affects our socialization—being told where we do or do not fit) can play a large part in determining whether we have a solidarity ethnic identity. We may also experience this posture depending on where we live, which family members we're close to, and what accents and/or languages we have.

Frank is an African American father with ethnically mixed kids. Having married a White woman, he is very focused on working against White normativity in their home and community. As an act of holy defiance on his part, and as an act of solidarity/allyship by his wife, they've chosen to raise their children in a solidarity-identity posture. While there will be space for the kids to further explore their ethnicities as they age (and they're certainly aware that their mom is White), the world mostly perceives them as people of color. It's important for them to understand Black culture and all that comes with being Black in America.

York is African American and European American but also identifies as Black. He's also in an interracial marriage to a White woman, but even in his multiethnic skin and multicultural family, he's still always felt "known, accepted, and celebrated" in Black culture, but "tolerated at best and rejected at worst" in majority-culture spaces. For us mixed folks, it's so important to find welcoming communities. For some of us, that tends to be in monoethnic circles. It's good to rest with other people who have common situations and experiences. If we mixed folks are constantly rejected by one of our cultures and accepted into another, it makes sense to be drawn into accepting communities. In a solidarity-identity posture, there can be a greater sense of belonging and a decrease in disconnect.

For those of us who can "pass" as majority-culture, there's an instant increase in privilege. For those of us who look "fully ethnic," the decrease in privilege and increase in discrimination is offset (somewhat) by the ability to persevere in community and to lament together. Some of us may even find wholeness in choosing to identify with a larger category of race: Latinx, Asian, Native, etc., or in choosing a specific national group, such as Ghanaian, Belizean, or Iranian.

But we must also acknowledge that when in this solidarity posture, there is the possibility of a sense of loss or of inauthenticity. Within our family, we may need to work through guilt, rejection, or embarrassment. We may lose the language, family customs, and other traditions of our non-emphasized culture. If we have lighter-skinned privilege and set it aside, there may be a sense of exhaustion or even self-doubt. Or, if we can "pass" and so we choose that privilege, there's the danger of buying into the ideals of monoethnicity. And there's the risk of denigrating a culture that is a part of ourselves.

But those of us who can look or act monoethnic don't need to be ashamed. Remember, our ethnicity is a gift from the Lord. It is simply a gift to be stewarded, as with all of God's gifts. In a solidarity-identity posture, we may be uniquely able to pursue justice and reconciliation. When we are strong enough, reminding monoethnic siblings that it isn't a Black-and-White world, through sharing our own experiences, can be a true gift.

For good identity formation and healthy self-care, the opportunity to step into monoethnic spaces can sustain us in our Christian walk. As long as we're honest with ourselves and open to what the Holy Spirit is doing, we can inhabit a solidarity-identity posture with confidence and authenticity.

Posture 2: shifting identity. When in this posture, we may seem like chameleons, able to change appearance and actions to blend almost seamlessly with our surroundings. We may "shift" on a regular basis or only in certain situations. Growing up in two or more cultures, having multiple family ties, and being multilingual can be factors, as well as being "racially ambiguous," which can allow access to more spaces. Being in this posture is largely affected by our phenotype and temperament, but we may find ourselves in the role of mediator or creative interpreter. The way others perceive us affects how we experience the world. There is no mixed "peacemaker" or "creative" gene, but our mixed experiences do tend to shape us in seeing others with creativity and kindness.

Melody, who describes herself as "half Mexi-talian and half stereotypically White," enjoys being able to identify with multiple cultures. Melody knows her maternal grandfather experienced past discrimination (being labeled "undesirable" in the post-WWI immigration era), so she's grateful that her Italian heritage and family has persevered through adversity. But in the current political climate, she chooses to "tell people that I'm Mexican before I tell them my other ethnicities because I want them to know who they're talking to and who they're talking about . . . that 'those people' are my people." Like Frank, Melody has a God-given heart for the marginalized, but her strong "Mexi-talian" identity means that in her pursuit of justice, she tends to identify with one ethnic affiliation and then another, to be in a shifting-identity posture.

Heidi Durrow, a Danish and African American novelist who refers to herself as an "Afro-Viking," has founded multiple festivals, foundations, and awards in which to honor and highlight the stories of mixed folks. She has worked with mixed folks like activist Willy Wilkinson, novelist Jamie Ford, and actor-producers Jordan Peele and Keegan-Michael Key. In their 2012 sketch-comedy show *Key & Peele*, the two introduce themselves as "half Black, half White, and particularly adept at lying because on a daily basis we have to adjust our blackness." It's a great punchline, but it's also a painful reminder that we mixed folks regularly have to adjust how we present our ethnicities.

Durrow created the festival to unite people in the mixed experience. In an interview with Leah Donnella, she laments that we mixed folks "haven't shared a sense of collective consciousness—and the art and scholarship that come with it—as long as other identity groups . . . [even though multiethnicity] 'has been happening from the beginning of this country.'"[4] She feels what many of us mixed folks feel: the need to have a space to talk about our experiences, to celebrate and process them through creative endeavors, to tell our mixed stories to the world.

One of the joys of being in this shifting-identity posture is the potential ability to build bridges and to bring God's understanding, healing, and true peace into a fractured situation. We also have our own cultural artifacts to share: our stories embodied as dance, art, poetry, and many other creations. When we're skilled in the art of code-switching with authenticity and intentionality, we can also be a real gift to the church as we seek to care for the marginalized and to break down artificial barriers. In the shifting-identity posture, we don't have to be good liars; we can be skilled truth-tellers instead.

But one possible pitfall of being in this posture is losing sight of ourselves, of becoming performance driven. We also may be accused of inauthenticity and culturally appropriating our own heritage. I've started to wonder if we mixed folks could use a secret handshake so we can always identify each other. I have certainly judged others harshly, thinking they were monoethnic. Because I didn't know their story, I assumed they were being fake in their choices of style or speech. I think that many of us have. Even if we make assumptions supposedly free from judgment, we're still missing out on knowing someone on a deeper level, of finding an ally and a friend. The irony is that mixed folks—those of us who may appear to be appropriating culture—are usually the most sensitive to, and judgmental of, the appearance of others doing it.

When we are in this shifting-identity posture, it's important to evaluate our influences and our motivations. We must ask, "Did I wear that headscarf because it's part of who I am, or to prove something to others?" "Am I including Middle Eastern elements in my wedding out of a sense of obligation or tokenism, or because I want to delve further into my heritage?" "Am I choosing to retire on a reservation because I want to be with my people, or because I feel guilty that I initially 'got out'?" The answers will be different for each of us, and they may even change in different seasons. So we do the work of continually drawing near to the Lord to hear and to apply his truth.

Posture 3: substitute identity. When in this posture, we aren't searching for a false utopian ideal of colorblindness; rather, for us mixed folks, it's a posture of finding community and healthy identity in areas other than our ethnicity. When we are in this posture, we don't identify as much (nor are we as affected by) the ways in which our differing ethnicities are distilled. We may choose this substitute-identity posture often, or we may find ourselves in this posture only with certain affinity groups. For those of us who were raised in a family that emphasized identity in a community, such as school activities, Scouting, or church, this may be a more natural posture. If our family of origin didn't discuss race much or acknowledge multiethnicity as a category, or if we are in mostly monoethnic (either

minority- or majority-culture) community, we may find ourselves in this category more often. In some ways, this is an
extension of the second posture, as we identify with one
identity and then another. The difference lies in whether or
not we set matters of ethnicity (mostly) aside.

I'm a woman of color, with Thai and European roots. This
is a huge part of my identity. And I was raised by a Black
father, so the African diaspora narrative is important to me.
But I also really love science fiction. When I'm in this substitute-identity posture, matters of ethnicity come up sometimes, but in those moments when I'm geeking out over *Star
Trek* or *Agents of S.H.I.E.L.D.*, I'm primarily enjoying being
a fan with likeminded folks. In these instances, my ethnicity
doesn't become irrelevant, but it does become peripheral to
my experiences. When there is ethnic diversity in a particular
community, it's either an established norm or a pleasant surprise. The majority of my interest, however, is captured by the
situations and characters of the show or book.

Brandee, who identifies as Black and White biracial, talks
about how her mixed experience informs how she leads
worship and also about how the worship team's shared love
of music is the primary focus of their time together. When
she's leading worship, she doesn't lose sight of her ethnicity,
but she enters a substitute-identity posture in which she feels
"really grateful to be able to serve." Even as she's leading songs
in different languages and styles, she's "not boxed in to one
way of worship, [but embraces] the fluidity of different
seasons of life." When she's raising her voice in praise,
appreciating the skills of her fellow musicians, and rejoicing
in hearing others worshiping in the congregation, her

substitute-identity posture allows her to "step into the fullness of who God created me to be."

The potential joy in this substitute-identity posture is being able to suspend a heightened awareness of ethnicity for at least a time. This is a privilege that monoethnic folks have—certainly White folks but also (at least to some extent) mono-ethnic minorities. When we're surrounded by people who look, act, and sound like us, differences can fade away, being replaced by a sense of harmony in common goals, interests, and experiences.

The rest, care, and energy that we can receive in such a space is invaluable. For a while, we're no longer *the other*. This isn't a privilege to be taken lightly; and for healthy, sustainable justice work, it's also not one to be scorned. A community that really bonds over mutual interests can feel welcoming and inclusive, no matter what ethnicities are represented.

The potential pitfalls of being in a substitute-identity posture are losing sight of the goodness of ethnicity, de-faulting to a White normativity, or losing touch with the goodness of the embodied Jesus as being from a particular ethnicity and culture. It can also take more effort to break out of the assumptions that others will make of us based on our appearance. Whether we desire to experience the world through a racial lens or not, the world will experience us in that way and will act according to its own stereotypes and suspicions.

When we find ourselves in this posture, we must strive not to listen to falsehoods but to push away unhealthy guilt, which may tell us that we're "selling out" or being false or unrealistic. "Self-care" is a trendy topic these days, and there are both gems of truth and shards of lies in the idea. As multiethnic people, we can love a multiethnic community well only if we are in the process of being whole in our multiethnic selves. So when we find a place of refuge, we should rest in it. These two realities are in tension, not in contradiction. We can be whole in our multiethnicity while still focusing on other aspects of our personhood. This is something usually afforded to monoethnic folks, so why not us mixed folks?

Crosscultural researcher Nakita Valerio has an important reminder about this serving/being served dynamic: "Shouting 'self-care' at people who actually need 'community care' is how we fail people."[5] Her words have really stuck with me. When we find communities that care for us well, we realize how essential others are to our health in body, spirit, and mind. Our embodied existence isn't meant to be lived alone. We aren't designed to be isolated—even those of us that are by nature introverts. And being multiethnic can be, by its very nature, isolating and lonely.

Society and our own doubtful hearts may whisper the lie that we'll never be accepted as we are, but the gospel loudly shouts the truth in response: in all of our varying identities— in ethnicity, in gender, in sexuality, in personality, in ability, and in experience, we are loved by God in all of who we are. And multiethnic folks have every right and privilege to explore the entirety of who God has made us to be, that we might rest in him and better serve his people.

Posture 4: singular identity. We find ourselves in this posture when we want to embrace a story of "both/and." In many circles, this singular-identity posture has been held up as the ideal for mixed folks—a place to finally "arrive" at. It isn't so simple, however. Throughout the Four Postures model, there's fluidity in when, how, and to whom a posture is most accurate. The heart behind it isn't to put anyone (or ourselves) in a box but rather to find a way of putting words to our experiences, to find ways to share our stories with each other. A both/and goal is important, but in some ways unattainable—at least on this side of heaven. Until our true identity in Christ is fully realized and fully reconciled, until we see him face to face, we'll continue to wrestle with who we are and who God has created us to be.

Tiffany is multiethnic (German American and Chinese Canadian) and a crosscultural adoptee (raised by a White family). She says, "To be mixed feels exhausting sometimes. . . . I wish I could be in a category. People say you can't be both, but I know what it means to be *othered*." For many of us, one common denominator to the mixed experience is one of isolation and exclusion, so finding a way to blend our ethnicities can be very healing. But often, being asked to be "all of who we are" is exhausting.

Joshua, who is Black, Asian, and White, has always seen his family members present 100 percent of their ethnicity, so he practices that too. He enjoys embracing this both/and dynamic, especially as he desires authenticity in all areas of life. Seeing himself as a blend of all his ancestors' cultures gives him encouragement as he thinks about the importance of family, geography, and belonging. He also admits that the language of "blended" and "authentic" must be handled carefully, as trying to be whole and "fully all" of his ethnicities can be an exercise in futility.

Rather than meeting others' expectations of how he should fully embody his varying heritage, Joshua chooses to blend them into one that's uniquely himself, to embrace a singular-identity posture. In this posture, he still must work to wisely avoid the expectation put on many of us mixed folk to add up to "100 percent." We're often pressured by well-meaning folks who don't realize that because we are not any one ethnicity, it may take 200 percent (or even 300 or 400 percent) of the work to get there.

The potential joys of being in this posture are a sense of wholeness and of being truly ourselves. When we embrace the both/and of the singular-identity posture, we're able to present ourselves cohesively to others, which means we can create a new culture and find solidarity with others. Blending our various identities can be a relief because we don't have to feel that we're choosing one part of ourselves over another. Speaking "Spanglish" or a similar blend of heart languages can show honor to who we are and to our upbringing. Blending the various aspects of our mixed ethnicity can be a valuable way to develop our personality and to share our unique culture with friends and family members.

A potential pitfall of being in this singular-identity posture is turning "wholeness" into an ideal—and thus an idol. The celebrated American melting pot of bland, assimilated cultural norms shows how blended singular-identity postures can result in a creamy White nothingness. In contrast, for those people whose European American heritage is now lumped under the catchall of whiteness, it can be a beautiful thing to move away from homogeneity and see specific parts of that heritage redeemed. Even as we press into reconciliation, we mixed folks have the opportunity and the privilege of not losing our own multiethnicity to mere whiteness or to other monoethnic cultures—even as we value, honor, and protect those other cultures.

After doing this heavy work of parsing our identities, finding which of the four postures are best for us in which circumstance, and receiving and speaking truth, we may be exhausted. As we think about the times we are in the *solidarity-identity posture* of identifying monoethnically, we can find rest in realizing that we're experiencing how "God . . . was at work in Peter as an apostle to the circumcised" (Gal 2:8). Peter depended on Jesus' forgiveness and the sustaining presence of the Holy Spirit to delve into his Jewish heritage and proclaim Christ. This is also our goal.

When we evaluate the times we've been in the *shifting-identity posture* of code-switching, we can be comforted that we've been like that other great apostle, Paul, who strove to "become all things to all people" (1 Cor 9:22) for the good of the kingdom. Just as he trusted God, no matter his circumstances, and adapted to the situation, we can also cling to Jesus as we are flexible in our identity.

The occasions that we're in a *substitute-identity posture*, focusing on something other than ethnicity, we can be reassured that we aren't merely in denial. Paul found a mutual affinity with Priscilla and Aquila "because he was a tentmaker as they were, he stayed and worked with them" (Acts 18:3), letting their mutual skills be part of their mission. Even as Paul both embraced and looked beyond his ethnic pedigree, we too can focus on different parts of our identity, some of which will have nothing to do with our ethnicity.

And when we look at the times we've been in a *singular-identity posture* of blending our ethnic story, we can remember that our inheritance isn't based on our mixed nature but on the multiethnicity of the Messiah, because "there is neither Jew nor Gentile . . . for you are all one in Christ Jesus" (Gal 3:28). No matter where we find ourselves, God is there with us. When we seek to follow the *ultimate* posture—one of service, sacrifice, and submission as exemplified in Jesus— we find joy wherever we are.

PART THREE OF THE MULTIETHNIC IDENTITY DISCIPLESHIP CYCLE: APPLY TRUTHS TO THE CHRISTIAN WALK

With the posture of the servant King, we look toward re-entering the first part of our discipleship cycle: prayer. But before we "start over," we complete this leg of our journey with part three of the cycle: we apply the truths we've learned to our Christian walk, expecting God to give us rest. Our rest may be literal, as we feel the impact our spiritual work has on our bodies. For example, I'm a big fan of naps. Depending on where we fall on the introvert-to-extrovert scale, the homebody-to-explorer scale, or the book-reading-to-sports-playing scale, we experience bodily rest differently. However we're wired, it's so important to remember that the human body is designed to work, but also to sleep and play— to sabbath.

It's also helpful to use spiritual practices such as the Examen,[6] a reflective prayer that can help us seek clarity in God's presence throughout the day. Before we dive back into asking the Lord questions about who we are in our ethnicity, we can rest in Jesus, our elder sibling and friend. Even as Jesus went away into the wilderness to seek time with his father, we have the privilege of joining him and drawing near to God.

Then we can think about our hopes for doing this often-difficult work of pressing into our multiethnic stories. Before we explore our role in our families and communities, our churches and society, we need to ensure that we're caring for ourselves well. Before we move into a discussion of how people of multiethnicity fit into a larger community and how we can serve others, we need to have resources and strategies to be intentional in developing our identity in Christ and in seeing it play out in everyday life.

It's important to circle back around to these foundational identity exercises and to pray without ceasing that we'll understand our identity in Christ. Whether you're a Christian going on several decades of belief and service, a newborn Christian at the beginning of a lifelong journey, or a skeptic questioning who this supposedly mixed Jesus person is; whether you're fairly comfortable with your multiethnicity or wary of it; whether you've spent years intentionally walking the mixed journey or are just now figuring out that you even "qualify" as a person of multiethnicity and all the implications therein, Jesus wants to tell all of us something. He's showing us who we are, why he loves us, and what this means for our lives and communities. He has created each one of us with loving care and intentionality. "And they were lovely because he loved them," indeed.[7]

CHAPTER SEVEN

Mixed Identity in Our Families and Communities

"How does Black plus White make Chinese?" the young woman jokingly asked my parents.

When I was younger, I looked "fully" Asian, so the sight of me, my White mom, and my Black dad together definitely challenged folks' assumptions. This is one of the reasons I wasn't surprised when, as I mentioned earlier, that little boy asked why my daughter looked "like China." I had similar experiences growing up. When I was young, people often asked if I knew kung fu or karate. As I developed more proto-typical European facial features in my teenage years, comments shifted to how "exotic" I looked. Especially in contrast with my parents, it was clear that I was something else entirely. To most people, my family just didn't make sense.

A large part of our identity formation is in our family of origin. Those of us who have been blessed with a stable home that meets our essential needs of being loved and cared for (which certainly looks different in varying cultures and across differing times) can build on our foundational experiences of safety, belonging, and purpose as we move forward in life and into the world. We can use our sense of security as a framework through which to better understand God, ourselves, and the world around us.

As psychiatrist Grant Hilary Brenner reports, studies have shown that for those of us who have experienced severe trauma in childhood and/or at home, our path is less defined.[1] If we've grown up in situations of poverty, violence, or abuse, we have a loss and a wounding that longs for healing. As survivors of domestic abuse can share, a large part of growing and thriving means finding safety and security in new situations, according to therapist Ellen Boeder.[2] Thankfully we can still find loving "family"—and thus healing—in new circumstances and in nontraditional ways.

In our foundational multiethnic experiences, our biological and legal families are the primary influence. But when it comes to healing, belonging, and growing, many of us find a loving family beyond our family of origin. While no family is perfect, and trauma and sin are universal human experiences in this fallen world, having somewhere to call home in our formative years is an essential part of developing an understanding of who we are as adults.

Even in the most loving and functional homes, however, multiethnicity can be a factor of dysfunction, not because being mixed is unnatural or harmful, but because it defies established familial and social categories. These family experiences don't have to be the majority of interactions—or even overtly traumatic—to have an impact. Many of us mixed folks come from happy homes with caregivers who handled multiethnicity as best they could. And while there's a clear delineation between a truly abusive home and a healthy one, there's a lot of middle ground, leaving room for both joy and sadness in all families.

A unique aspect of being mixed is how our existence pushes against the binary thinking of the Western world. Simple categories are shown to be wanting, and family experiences are no exception. In a world that wants to categorize things as either wholly good or completely bad, we mixed folks are a walking reminder that not everything is so clear-cut.

THE FAMILY TIES THAT BIND (OR NOT)

Sundee Tucker Frazier dedicated *Check All That Apply* to "my brother, Isaac, because you understand."[3] When we grow up in a family with other multiethnic siblings, we can take great comfort in having someone else who understands the experience of living in one family and two (or more) different worlds. Having a sibling we can identify with can help with the sense of disconnect if we phenotypically match only one parent, or even look like neither parent.

Author Cindy Wilson also praises the loyalty of her brother. She's a crosscultural adoptee who cheerfully identifies as "Asian but my culture is Black."[4] In her book *Too Much Soul*, she expresses gratitude for her adopted brother, to whom she bears no physical resemblance. Rather than resenting her sibling who phenotypically matches their parents, she finds joy in knowing that her ethnically Black brother understands her in a way no one else can. Cindy, in her Korean skin, identifies with prototypical Black culture in some ways that he doesn't, so the fact that he also lives between two worlds gave a strong basis for their sibling bond. She says she "witnessed him struggle to fit in with different groups of people,"[5] and that helped her connect with him in a way she may not have otherwise. She says, "I was different because I looked different. I was an Asian child growing up with a Black family in the deepest part of the South. But my brother . . . he took the cake on actually being different."[6]

In addition to being raised together, they both appreciate the other for breaking stereotypes and knowing what it's like to explain oneself when appearance and actions don't meet other folks' standards. They know what it means to be the *other*, but also what it means to define oneself proudly as an individual side by side with another individual.

My mother told me in my teenage years that one of the reasons she and my dad never had a child together was because they didn't want to alienate me with a sibling who *did* look like them. I was grateful, but also grieved for what might have been—and also for my sinful reaction to the idea. In my childhood, I had pain because I looked like neither of my parents; so I have no doubt I would have struggled to relate to siblings who genetically—and thus most likely physically—belonged to them both.

As I think about it now, what grieves me the most is the loss of community I had in not being raised with siblings (nor with my half or stepsiblings from my parents' other marriages). If my parents had decided to have children within their marriage, those hypothetical siblings would have had their own struggles with multiethnicity, something we would have had in common. Though we would have been mixed with different ethnic backgrounds, we could have walked through that reality together.

But having siblings is no guarantee for us multiethnic folks. The ABC comedy *Mixed-ish* introduces the origin story of Rainbow, a mixed woman with a Black mother and White father. When she's twelve, her family leaves the sheltered, color-blind commune in which she was raised, and she suddenly must face the segregated culture of the 1980s. She laments a life in which "no one in the world is like you . . . not even your parents." Even her siblings can't empathize with her. Because of their phenotypical appearances, her younger brother is able to fit in with the Black kids, and her sister is able to align herself with the White kids. But Rainbow is unable to find a home in either camp.

BOXING THE *OTHER* IN

National Geographic magazine made a clear statement about the absurdity of racial profiling on the cover of its April 2018 special issue.[7] The cover photo featured fraternal twin girls who, though both mixed Jamaican and English (White) with the same parents, would be classified very differently from each other based on appearance: one looks White and the other Black.[8]

The increasing number of us "openly" mixed folks has helped to shine light on the reality that race is indeed a social construct, not a biological reality. When looking at sisters who appear to be of two different races *although they are twins*, we start to realize the impact of racial-ization, which, as Daniel Lee explains, is the reality of outsiders declaring what race someone is.[9] This signifi-cantly affects all people, and us multiethnic folks espe-cially. Author Jemar Tisby reminds us that lines of race (as constructed based on appearance) have always been, and continue to be, used to separate "us" from "them."[10] We mixed people, who complicate that process, can be a threat to either side.

A COMPLICATED LEGACY

For some of us mixed folks, we feel little disconnect within our family of origin but much awkwardness within our broader extended family. If we experienced our household as a close-knit community, we may be able to find ourselves comfortable with who we are. But it's a foundational aspect of the multiethnic experience to have some measure of being not quite at home, no matter how we define home. Whether we're being outright rejected by extended family or insidiously celebrated by them for having more "attractive" features (meaning light-skinned and White-normative), extended family can be a difficult circumstance even in monoethnic situations. So our multiethnicity can further complicate extended-family relationships.

Steve has a unique perspective, being mixed Latino and White, as well as having married a White woman. Growing up, his *tias* "preferred me to my darker-skinned siblings because of colorism. [Now, these aunties have also] fawned over my light-skinned kids." This is the "Great-Grandma Gertrude Factor," as Sundee Frazier puts it,[11] in which negative interactions with extended family can affect mixed-race marriages and their children. Our experiences can range from a having a painful coexistence with extended family members to being overtly excluded, and everything in-between.

Negative family interactions also can affect people several generations down the line. Jessie, who has a White mom and a Black dad, said,

> One of the most shocking things my mother ever said to me was an offhanded statement while I was in college. She told me that she hoped I didn't fall in love with a Black man. It was one of those moments where you wonder what science-fiction alternate reality you've found yourself in. I frantically thought: *Is my mom actually a White supremacist? Did I miss something here? Am I in a Dave Chappelle sketch? Why on earth wouldn't she be okay with me marrying a Black man the way she did?*

While marrying interracially is certainly no proof of being nonracist (and may even be a hindrance in the active work of being *anti-racist*, Robin DiAngelo reminds us[12]), Jessie was relieved to hear her mom clarify what she meant: "She said she wanted to spare me the pain of our extended family's lack of support. 'It's been such a painful journey for your dad and me,' she said, 'and I don't want you to have to experience that.'"

The irony, of course, is that by Jessie's mom having children in an interracial marriage, she created an entire lineage of interracial marriages. Hopefully further generations will be more accepting, but because Jessie's maternal grandparents didn't approve of their daughter's mixed marriage, they missed out on much of their grandchildren's childhoods. For many majority-culture folks, outsiders being of another race is one thing; it is quite another when the "outsider" is in the family.

When it comes to legacy, passing on culture and values can be complicated for any family. In our mixed families, there's an extra layer of complexity. Karen often feels lonely "because there is no way to have ethnic traditions passed down to me in my multiethnicity," in both her White and Middle Eastern heritages. Each of her parents can present her with different cultural norms and traditions, but it's up to her (and her sisters) to figure out how to integrate each culture into multiethnic life. As she and her siblings determine which multiethnic traditions to pass along, it can be tiring.

There also may be grief about what has been lost. Bethany, in her Latina and White heritage, laments that because the Latino side of her family assimilated to the dominant culture of the United States, "there's a part of my family history I'll never know." She wonders, "How do I connect with a culture that I know nothing about?"

While our extended family can be a source of trauma, it also can be a place where God speaks life to us. Kristina, with her Latina and White ancestry, found some healing by visiting her extended family in Mexico. Because she doesn't speak Spanish fluently, her grandmother was there to translate for her. She asked her *abuela* to tell the rest of the family she was "grateful for letting me be part of their family, for letting me come." Her aunt's response brought Kristina to tears: "*No, mija—tú* eres *familia!*" ("No, sweet child, you *are* family!") Despite her limitations in speaking Spanish and sometimes feeling "lesser" than her brother, who looks more phenotypically Latino, Kristina is finding healing in being called "daughter," in being accepted and loved by family members who speak the truth that she *is* family.

Family—and the ways in which family members do and do not meet our expectations—changes how we perceive ourselves. Having been raised solely in the United States, I've often felt disconnected from my Asian heritage. Meeting my extended Thai family in my thirties meant a lot, and finally walking on Thai soil was formative for me. It is soil in which my ancestors are buried, soil on which those ancestors once walked. Until my trip to Thailand, I'd never had the privilege of being in a room full of people with whom I had genetic ties, who looked like me. It was incredibly affirming, even though I still felt awkward in my very non-Thai language, habits, and culture.

Spending time with my Black family feels very natural, though it can have its awkward moments. Although I don't look like them, I feel very comfortable in terms of shared humor and experiences; I code-switch both in terms of speech and mannerisms. Though my family obviously knows my story, if we're out in public, there can be stares from all sorts of people.

Interactions with both of these extended family groups are good, and they're helpful to me as I explore more of my multi-cultural and multiethnic reality. These experiences aren't in competition; they are both valuable. Because my Thai and Black families are both welcoming and loving in their own ways, time with them helps me to understand myself better than just spending time with my family of origin ever could. But it's still not easy to feel that I fit in.

HEALING BROKENNESS, REDEEMING IDENTITY

A sense of alienation can be pervasive for us mixed folks, and the emphasis on differences starts early. When Aton, who has African American, Mexican, and Native roots, was a child, he saw an old snapshot of his grandmother with a child in her lap. He asked her, "Who's that White baby you're holding?" He received the answer that it was him. So Aton learned from an early age that he could be seen as the plot twist, the jarring reality that explains everything else. Even with a loving family, he internalized the idea that he was the exception to his family's rule, the misfit.

Krista, with her Vietnamese and White heritage, felt that lack of belonging from an early age. But she didn't know how to articulate it until her midtwenties, when she "had space to be challenged and to process." She said, "Ethnicity shapes so much of who I am. . . . I grew up in a Vietnamese immigrant church and that has influenced my view of God." Now she's able to push back on the lie that she doesn't fit.

Being a mismatch is a lie we're all susceptible to. It's rooted in Adam and Eve's failure in the Garden of Eden, a lie that says we aren't enough. It's a lie that's whispered in our ears: "God made a mistake with you. And the only way to fix it is to change who you are, to be someone else." As with all lies, it takes a lot of effort to speak truth to ourselves again and again, to embrace ourselves as mixed folks in the way that God embraces us.

Wrestling with identity is something that allies such as adoptees and those in blended and/or crosscultural families can empathize with; it's a common theme that many multicultural folks share. Those with vitiligo and albinism can also walk with us mixed folks as we figure out what embodied identity in Christ actually means. In 2017, I had the honor of recording a StoryCorps segment with my friend KeNosha, who has albinism. As a self-proclaimed "golden girl," she tells people she's "a Black woman trapped in a White woman's body." She knows what it's like to struggle to celebrate the melanin of Black and Brown brothers and sisters while still celebrating the skin tone God has given her. She says her albinism "caused me to look drastically different from my family, and I had some issues with that growing up surrounded by this beautiful brown skin [of my family members]."

She and I can empathize and celebrate with each other. Though not the same, our experiences have some commonalities that allow us to be allies and friends. We mixed folks can care well for each other—and for monoethnic folks—in community by speaking truths of belonging and welcome, even as we acknowledge our differences.

"BUT WHAT ABOUT THE CHILDREN?"

When mixed marriage was made legal, one of the arguments against it was "But don't the children suffer?" Drawing on the tragic-mulatto myth, majority-culture folks made the claim that biracial children would suffer so greatly that mixed marriages were a bad idea. Rather than seeing nuanced stories of differing families and experiences, they lumped all of us multiethnic folks into one tragic group.

While rejecting the lie that all people of multiethnicity are a monolith, psychologist Beverly Daniel Tatum also doesn't reinforce an unhelpful binary. While discussing dependable research on the development of biracial children, she points out that "while it is clear that biracial children can grow up happy and healthy, it is also clear that particular challenges associated with a biracial identity must be negotiated. . . . The existence of the biracial person challenges the rigid boundaries between Black and White."[13]

So while it's true that we multiethnic folks aren't destined for misery, we do have some common struggles. "The importance of the parents' role in helping children make sense of the . . . race-related experiences they are having, cannot be overemphasized," says Daniel Tatum.[14] Those parents who are people of color understand some of the complexities their children face, but not all. They have to be humble and proactive in ensuring that their children can talk about issues of race from a variety of perspectives. It's very important for minority parents of multiethnic children to realize that they will never completely understand their children's experiences, even as they can identify with growing up as a person of color. As they share their own experiences of race in a world that tries to de-value the *other*, minority parents of mixed kids can be a real source of comfort in helping expand the narrative and norms that their children are already pushing back against.

If majority-culture parents are in the family mix, another level of intentionality and selflessness is required. I like to refer to these folks as "parents of color" or "parents of multiethnicity," because although they won't experience multiethnicity themselves, they'll share some of the mixed experience through the lives of their children. Those parents who work hard to understand their child's perspective and to honor their ethnic culture will feel issues of injustice and disconnect keenly on their children's behalf.

Continuing her interview with Leah Donnella, activist Heidi Durrow said, "'I feel like my mom gets to be as mixed as I do . . . ' when, say, visiting a Black history museum with her White mother, she worries that some may see her mom as an intruder. In those moments, she says, 'I always want to wrap my arms around my mom and make sure people know that . . . she's connected to me. And that matters.'"[15] Heidi knows that her mom sees the world differently than she used to, that part of her motherhood is now wrapped up in an ethnicity not her own.

Emily, who is White with Black biracial children, shares how humbling being a parent in a multiethnic family can be. She says she realizes—such as when she thinks about doing her daughters' hair—"I can't be everything to them. And that's a good thing." Being a parent of mixed kids has required her to parent in community, to reach out to others to help her figure out how to take good care of Black/mixed hair. More importantly, she realizes that, in her pale skin, she isn't enough to help her children figure out their brown-skinned identity. She says they need to have "wise Black women in their lives" so they can be surrounded by an affirmation of their ethnicity and can have other women to discuss what being a Black woman in America looks like. Emily is serving her children by admitting that she can't meet all their needs. It's a lesson all parents and leaders could benefit from.

And for some of us multiethnic folks, as we contemplate having children, we can see how even that journey is a new one. In addition to being ethnically Black and Latino, Aton is also close to an Asian family with which he identifies culturally. Now that he has married a White woman, he often thinks about how each generation will change, and he wonders what it will be like to "learn this new space and this new identity with our kids." Even though he is himself mixed, he realizes that each successive generation will have journeys different from those of their parents.

I have to admit I lament that my sweet daughters are "only" a quarter Thai. Their phenotypically Asian features are fading as they grow older, especially in the younger of the two, who favors her dad in appearance. I did not marry Tiger Woods (which is a blessing for a number of reasons), but I used to like to harass my White husband by telling him, "Tiger Woods and I would have had beautiful children: about a third Thai, a third Black, and a third White." That was almost twenty years ago. Now that I've grown in my own ethnic identity and my children have been born (and after Woods's painful scandal and subsequent divorce), I don't make that joke anymore. But I have to be honest that I still struggle with the diminishing of my Asian heritage that I see in my girls' faces. And this is in the context of my fight against my own internalized colorism—a preference for medium-toned skin and blended features. Even while I long for them to look more Thai, I have to admit that I'm unhealthily pleased they've got that "mixed" appearance.

So I have repent for my fetishizing of mixed babies, a practice rooted both in the fear that White folks can have of dark skin and in the exhaustion we multiethnic folks have in our "minorities of minorities" status. I have to admit that in my twenties, I had a strange way of accepting my knowledge that my future children would probably experience some of the same loneliness I faced. It played out in a self-deprecating, defeatist attitude of "well, my kids may get made fun of, but at least they'll be cute."

In parenting these theoretical children now turned flesh, it has been interesting to watch them navigate their own similarities and differences. While obviously siblings, they are phenotypically different in how much of their Asian heritage is evident. I love watching big sister enjoy her dark hair while appreciating her younger sister's lighter shade. I'm grateful for when little sister compliments her older sister on her freckles without denigrating her own rosy cheeks. Even while they have much in common, their bond as siblings is powerful, not in spite of their differences but because of them.

ALL IN THE FAMILY

Even as I say this, I want to repent publicly of my own colorism and of how I've been part of the problem. I encourage all of us mixed folks to repent of the ways in which we've judged others, even while we admit that we don't have all the answers. We are not the embodiment of the answer to discrimination. Jesus is that answer, and while his multiethnicity is part of his reality, it isn't the entirety of it.

Yes, Jesus' lineage is an important part of who he is. But in terms of our identity in Christ, what matters most is who he is as our prophet, priest, and king. Jesus repented *for us* and *became sin* for us—which includes all our hatred of self and others (2 Cor 5:21), and he put that to death. That's the real hope for us, our families, and indeed all the world.

Family members don't have to look, sound, or even act alike to be family. For a genetic family, the bonds are in blood; for a legal family, the bonds are in ink. But even those relationships still have to be forged through mutual love, acceptance, and shared experience. For those of us who have found family in our groups of friends, we've been drawn together by some shared characteristic, whether visible or not. And in terms of the family of God, we are bound together not by our own work but by the redeeming work of Jesus and the healing work of the Holy Spirit. That is something we can depend on.

CHAPTER EIGHT

Mixed Identity in the Church and Society

I AM
The blood of Anglo colonizers
The tears of Cherokee mothers
The sweat of Brown trabajadores

Love and Violence
Sit at my Table
Privilege and Powerlessness
Stare back at me in the mirror

HUMBLE RECONCILER
PRINCIPE DE PAZ
Teach us to be family

CHRISTINA MARIE QUINTANILLA, "PRAYER OF A MIXED WOMAN"[1]

As we think of the hope that we have in Jesus, we move from our innermost circle of influence—close family—and into the sphere of our universal family: the church. Some of us are blessed to have our family of origin and current family as part of Christ's body—a double family tie. Some of us have family members who aren't believers, and thus we don't share that specific bond. Either way, for us mixed folks, there's often a longing to find a community that reflects the diversity of the general human experience, in addition to our specific life experiences. Family is foundational but can also be alienating. Having grown up in a loving situation, I still felt a disconnect with those at home, at school, and among my friends. I often felt like a misfit, and not just when things were difficult. Sometimes I felt most disconnected during the best of times, as that contrast highlighted my differences. This tension didn't lessen in my teen years and into college, even as the pressures of academic and social success loomed large.

And then there was church.

BODY BROKEN

I started my Christian walk in college, in a church with wonderful, caring people who welcomed a very rough-around-the-edges me. I was baptized in that church, learned hymns in that church, and pushed boundaries and received forgiveness in that church. There was acceptance and love for almost every part of me—even the scary, sinful parts. But there wasn't much diversity nor an understanding of how being a minority of any kind—especially a person of color who is mixed—complicates one's relationship with mono-ethnic institutions. The church where I first "walked the aisle" to confess my sins and later walked the aisle to be married met many of my needs. But that dear church where I learned about service and sacrifice didn't meet a fundamental need I had: to explore the significance of my ethnicity. I needed to be able to see God's hand in making me multiethnic—not as a mistake, but as part of my calling and service.

I needed a multiethnic church.

Really I needed "the church to be the church," as my friend, historian Otis Pickett, would say. The church universal was, is, and will be multiethnic, throughout history and beyond. The past four hundred years of church division in the United States are the anomaly, neither the kingdom goal nor the universal church norm.

Anyone who challenges the majority-culture American standard of the monoethnic (White) church can get a variety of responses. To that pushback, I'll agree that yes, it's important to have diversity that mirrors the community, and not just diversity for diversity's sake. But just because a neighborhood is mostly White doesn't mean that a church gets a pass for having no diversity. Yes, tokenism shouldn't be the means nor the end goal for a church. But there's a difference between the tokenism of allowing a few people of color in and expecting them to assimilate (to appease some ethereal goal of diversity) and bringing people of color into leadership and letting them make significant changes for good. And even in all-White communities, there's often a lot more diversity in a given area than what majority-culture folks see or acknowledge, especially when it comes to us mixed folks. What White church leaders often don't realize is that if there are few (or no) people of color in a church, it's probably not because we aren't available.

More likely, it's because we don't feel comfortable or seen—in the entirety of our embodied selves—in that space. A rigidly monocultural church misses out on fellowship with people of color because we aren't welcomed in our entirety. But churches can also lose out on the joy and giftings of mixed folks when we, out of self-protection, can't actively identify as multiethnic in church settings. Because we're forced to "choose sides" and identify monoethnically, the main burden is on the church, not on mixed individuals, to make changes.

In many majority-culture churches, people of color are welcomed but are also expected to assimilate culturally. While I was definitely welcomed into my first church family, I was expected to behave in certain ways, many of which were not biblical mandates, but simply cultural preference. Church culture—what is and isn't acceptable—forms through a lens of normativity, and that sweet church was no exception. The difficulty is, White churches often don't think of themselves as having a specific culture, in the same way that we humans tend to see other folks as the ones with an accent, not ourselves. When any people group starts with the assumption that it is the norm and everyone else is the aberration, not only are dividing walls put up where there should be none, but those walls are very difficult to tear down.

I'll also acknowledge that, addressing pushback I've heard before, trying to integrate groups with different primary languages can be difficult (in the case of my hometown, that's mostly English-speaking White folks and Spanish-speaking

Hispanic peoples). Still, this is clearly a challenge that God can and has overcome. We see this in God's global call in Isaiah 49, the coming of the Holy Spirit translator of Acts 2, and the glorious fulfillment of the multiethnic, multicultural, and multi*lingual* new heavens and new earth prophesied in Revelation 7 and 21. Basically we can look through the entire Bible and see the ways in which God has communicated with us—and allowed us to communicate with each other—across cultures. The "dividing wall of hostility" that Paul writes of (Eph 2:14) has been broken down and bridged across in the *multiethnic* body of Christ.

COMPARING APPLES TO MANGOES

We people of color know just how much majority-culture folks balk at criticisms leveled at their monoethnic churches by comparing their institutions to those of *minority* mono-ethnic church groups and organizations. If other groups get to be monoethnic, their reasoning goes, why can't we? As with general issues of race in society, the power dynamic is completely different between these two types of monoethnic churches. Historically Black denominations were created because slaves weren't allowed to worship in primarily White churches. Historian Tisby reminds us, "harsh though it may sound, the facts of history nevertheless bear out this truth: there would be no Black church without racism in the White church."[2]

And when we think carefully about ethnic-specific churches, such as Korean and Spanish congregations (really any church in America that conducts services in a language other than English), we realize the value of being able to worship in one's own "heart language." This is something that many English-speaking believers—myself included—take for granted.

For many indigenous believers in Christ, it's been essential to form their own Native churches where they can be free of the pressures to conform to White culture. Too many majority-culture church leaders, seemingly incapable of doing the biblical work of parsing culture from religion, go far past scriptural bounds in what they consider to be acceptable. While wisely acknowledging the danger of syncretism when integrating traditional cultural practices within the church, Rosebud Lakota/Sioux author Richard Twiss, in *One Church, Many Tribes: Following Jesus the Way God Made You*, shares several examples of Native believers being made to feel as though they had to give up every aspect of their culture to be Christians.

Within Native churches, there have always been deep discussions regarding what objects, traditions, and music can indeed be "adapted to sacred use."[3] This is not only wise and necessary, it goes back to the earliest traditions of Christianity. Twiss reminds us that

> in the Early Church, Paul warned new believers against continuing in certain practices *until they were spiritually strong enough* to see the *artificiality* of its tie to a former belief. Once they were able to do this, they could then clearly see meat for what [it] is—grub—and the idol for what it truly is—powerless sticks and stones (see Rom 14:1-23; 1 Cor 8:1-13).[4]

How quick humans are to forget that *all* cultures need to do this mental and spiritual work: to "test the spirits" (see

1 Jn 4:1-3) and to question cultural norms. More than this, how often we non-majority-culture folks have no choice but to either culturally assimilate or form our own groups and churches (at which point we're accused of being the difficult ones). True unity is not possible when the White church forces others into that false dichotomy.

FROM CULTURE TO CHURCH, AND BACK AGAIN

This interplay of cultural and ethnic realities is one reason for not excluding multi*cultural* issues from the scope of this book: we mixed folks can also struggle to feel a sense of belonging in terms of cultural norms. Even for those of us who are multiethnic minority/minority, with no explicitly majority culture family heritage, the clash usually comes from differing cultures rubbing up against each other.

Ultimately it's our experience with a larger group's reaction to us that leaves indelible marks of alienation. So school and other activities can become a key source of awkward, hurtful experiences. Adam, discussing his experiences as both Asian and Polish, said "Outside my house, such as in school, I really wasn't like anyone else, though my father always told me to check 'Chinese' when having to identify my race. I accepted and adopted this in-betweenness as my identity for many years."

Before the days where "Check all that apply" was available on forms, we mixed folks *had* to choose. There are many of us who currently choose to identify as one ethnicity; that is not the problem. To be *forced* to choose is the real issue. Having to value one part of ourselves over another, even when we're just trying to fill out seemingly innocuous insurance forms,[5] is hurtful and alienating.

We mixed folks are seen as anomalies that disrupt societal norms, both in our physical appearance and in our behavior. Even for those White folks who claim to have no problem with other ethnicities and who advocate for "Black and White" being "separate but equal," we multiethnic folks disrupt their very Black-and-White thinking with our existence as Black-White-and-other-ethnicities people.

Because of discriminatory anti-miscegenation laws which banned mixed marriages, we multiethnic folks who have White ancestry were born of an illegal union just fifty years ago. Many of us are well aware that our very presence is an affront to those who prefer general segregation, and especially to those who abhor mixed marriages. As many people throughout history can attest (and especially with current large waves of immigration), being labeled "illegal" is especially dehumanizing and cruel.

PROGRESS-*ISH* . . .

As our society learns more about rejecting colorblindness, there's a shift to wanting to see each and every skin tone valued in the entire spectrum: from folks with albinism to those with the most melanin, and every shade in-between. This is in direct contrast with the idea that culture and beauty must be "watered down" into a sad state of generic beige. And yet that is what mixed people are often made to represent. Multiethnic folks with a medium skin tone can be idolized by White folks who are frightened by dark skin and the cultures it represents.

We can also be seen as a risk to our Black and Brown siblings. For those with significant amounts of melanin,

White folks have always been an actual threat; our country is founded on the brutal treatment of those with non-European features and dark skin, and people of color are right to suspect whiteness, author Daniel Hill reminds majority-culture folks.[6] But we mustn't let the prospect of multiethnicity feed into the idea of purity for either light *or* dark skin. The *cultural ideals* of whiteness are toxic and can spread. But the human variety of skin tones is just one of God's good gifts.

This is true even when different skin tones come from a history not of unity, but of abuse and conquest. Many mixed indigenous folks' lineages involve stories of kidnappings and forced "marriages." Those of us with Asian heritage may have ancestors who were brought to America to be the brides (that is, "property") of White men. In terms of Black and White multiethnicity, some of the first mixed people in the United States were the children borne out of the rape of enslaved women by their "owners." Though many of us have sweet stories of how we are proof of reconciliation between different ethnicities, many of us do not.

And this has never been just a societal problem. Many of those brutal slave-owning men were described as "pillars" of the church. In discussing the KKK during the Jim Crow era, Tisby relates that "many Klan members actively participated in their local churches, and some of the same men who conducted night rides [terrorizing Black citizens] on Saturday ascended to the pulpit to preach on Sunday."[7]

As churches repent of a historical complicity with racism, they need to be reminded that mixed folks' presence in society isn't a simplistic solution, but that we can be a catalyst for changes to come. Our presence can also be a monument of change that has already occurred. Pastor Brenda Salter McNeil exhorts us to "build monuments . . . to mark what we have done and the small accomplishments we've made along the way."[8] We mixed-race folks can be living monuments to ancestors who persevered despite brutal treatment, to parents and grandparents who defied unhealthy societal conventions.

In our very flesh, we are "reminders of what God has done and the victories we have won [which] will lend us encouragement and strength on the road to reconciliation."[9] Part of our answer to the call of Romans 12:1 is to embrace the unique way in which we can "offer [our] bodies as a living sacrifice, holy and pleasing to God."

Despite the violence upon which our country's culture was founded, this is a lesson where current society is actually outdoing us. We in the church have been commanded to "honor one another above [our]selves" (Rom 12:10; some translations: "outdo one another in showing honor"), and thus to show the waiting world that they can trust that we are Jesus people by our love. But often we worry so much about what divides us that we lose sight of the God who unites us.

This isn't a simplistic Sunday school answer. We mixed folks can be one of the groups to show the church what it means to celebrate differences while maintaining unity. Despite the issues we face in society at large, our mixed existence is no mere frustration, no mere blip on the radar screen. If churches can get their priorities straight, we'll see that God is using us to speak truth to his church—and through her, we can then speak truth to the society around us.

OUT THERE AND IN HERE

It should come as no surprise to us that "out there" in the world, we mixed folks (and indeed, all people) can be ostracized and treated by others as difficulties to be overcome. What's truly heartbreaking, however, is how many of us identify the church as a place where we feel the most unseen or unwanted.

York has experienced racism in the church "more subtly" than in other spaces but still as very present. In his work consulting with churches that desire more multiethnicity, he asks for the promise of "a tithe from the organization"—that is, an agreement that at least 10 percent of their leadership is made up of people of color. As he says, you "can't have constructs divorced from people," and you "can't have change divorced from power."

This is very evident in majority-culture monoethnic churches. For most monoethnic churches made up of *minorities*, the church is a space in which to escape persecution, to not be treated as less than human, and to embrace unique languages and cultures. But many White churches are not unique; they simply *are*, as are all the majority spaces in the attendees' lives. When they invite minorities in, they don't realize that people of color are entering into a space where they're strongly *other*-ized. The needs and realities of us mixed folks add other layers of complexity that often seem to be asking "too much" of White congregations.

This is also why multi*ethnic* churches tend to be monocultural, as researcher Korie L. Edwards has found,[10] tending to end up with dominant-culture communication styles, worship practices, and concerns. Because our society is steeped in whiteness, without intentionality and repentance on the part of church leaders, even multiethnic spaces will skew toward majority-culture norms. So as part of their overall work against White normativity, church leaders need to be more intentional in caring for us multiethnic people and families. As temperament and energy permit, we who are multiethnic can help build bridges between two cultures.

Because of issues of colorism, where light-skinned people are seen as more valuable, some of us multiethnic people can be viewed as a "safer" alternative to those who have darker skin or less European features. We who are essentially "beige" are often used as a way for majority-culture leaders to highlight (pun very intended) the diversity that's supposedly already present, not as a tithe and promise of a church's commitment to diversity. Tokenism is taken to new extremes when beige folks are valued for their ability to visually appease both darker- and lighter-skinned members. If congregants are generally threatened by diversity, the hope is that they won't notice a more ambiguous-looking person. Or, if some are hoping for diversity, church leaders may attempt to mollify them with this supposed step of progress.

THE DYSTOPIAN MULTIETHNIC CHURCH

It's frustrating when majority-culture White churches dismiss and ignore the real concerns of people of color. Even more heartbreaking are the ways in which *multiethnic* churches and organizations can be a source of pain for us people of multiethnicity. Kylene, experiencing the world as Asian and White, is encouraged by some progress, but she still has "a lot of doubts as to whether or not the evangelical church will ever get it right."

Brandee elaborates on her experiences as a mixed Black and White woman, saying, "I never felt fully comfortable or included in evangelical space. It's such a bifurcated expression of Christianity: Black and White—literally and metaphorically; in and out; right and wrong. That never sat right with my both/and experience and worldview."

Bethany, considering her Latinx and White heritage, often wonders, "Why in multiethnic communities are the multiethnic people the ones who feel the most left out?" This is a painful question, and an important one. Even in my own organization, *multiethnic* as an identifier is applied to groups only, not to individual people. Multiethnicity has become synonymous with diversity, yet the idea of a diverse *person* is confusing in our bifurcated world.

But we mixed folks can be an encouragement to our churches, if they listen. Tiffany, in her identity as both mixed and a crosscultural adoptee, has found Jesus' promised strength in her weakness. The "struggle and dissonance" of her heritage and adoption story has allowed her to feel safe in "asking questions about who he is, and who I am," to press into relationship with the Lord.

As she has contemplated Psalm 1 and the image of the rooted tree, she has loved knowing that being rooted in Christ gives life and meaning to her and to all of her identities. "Everything that I am and that he's made me to be—life gets breathed into those identities," she says. Rather than worrying that asking questions will cause fear in her heart, she knows a willingness to see more than just "Black and White" and to sit in those tensions eases her fear, increases her trust in God, and informs her ability to serve the church.

FACING OUR DISCOMFORTS

Being multiethnic in a monoethnically focused world can be very uncomfortable. But God has not called us to be comfortable, and there is no shortage of controversy these days surrounding Westerners and our love of comfort. Ours is a culture that values accomplishments and having "arrived," whether in our home, work, or extracurricular pursuits. We aren't comfortable with discomfort. Our tendency to find shortcuts and to take the easy way out isn't just allowed; it's applauded. The Western evangelical church (very broadly defined) is no exception.

Though we travel as sojourners, the truth is that rather than impacting the world, many of our congregations have allowed themselves to be influenced by the society around us. In the Western world, our love of comfort and our love of security are intertwined, and things that confuse us aren't welcome. So we mixed folks can pose a threat to society at large and, more specifically, to the local church. Conversely, sometimes our presence is celebrated to an unhealthy extreme. Either way, we're seen as caricatures of ourselves, instead of real people. But when we push back, we can be agents of change.

Even with the recent rise in numbers of multiethnic churches, there is rarely a "Check all that apply" option in the highly segregated American churches of today. Lo, who is ethnically Native and European American and who culturally identifies mostly as White, feels the weight of the painful reality that religious groups (with some notable exceptions)

are mostly ignoring the issue of race and ethnicity, and especially when it comes to mixed people.

And with religious groups, appearance is often the only
indicator used to determine a person's identity. Every time Lo
speaks to a church or is on a panel and is identified as ethnically White, it's a struggle to know how to respond. Lo
wonders, "Is it worth it to correct them? Should I point it out?
Will people just judge me? Is it important that I correct
them?" For those of us mixed folks who are light-skinned and
have the ability to "pass" as White, it's critical that we remain
aware of this unfair advantage. But even this awareness can
further complicate the matter and bring more trauma, because guilt often accompanies our awareness of privilege.
And even as churches try to identify the "haves" and "have-
nots" to better bring people of color to the table, we mixed
folks are often either tokenized or overlooked.

Adam is an atheist, and shares that he "never really felt
at home at church" for several reasons, his Asian and White
multiethnicity definitely among them. The requirement
that he assimilate to the dominant culture made him feel
"out of sorts." Eventually, he decided, "I'm my own person.
I don't fit in over here, I don't fit in over there, I'm my own
thing." He left the church to look for more diverse and
accepting communities.

Chris, who is Black and White, identifies as "culturally
Christian" but is actually agnostic. Due to cultural expectations, he feels that his doubts are inherently tied up in his
multiethnicity. Given the strong ties of prototypical African
American culture with the church, he wonders, "Is it weird
that the more Christian I act the more Black I feel? Even

though I was raised in a primarily White church, that notion still gets me. It just feels like my lack of faith alienates me more from one side of my ethnic identity than the other." Rather than his church experiences helping him to better understand his multiethnicity and vice versa, they cause him to feel alienated and burdened by heavy expectations.

Kevin, an Asian American and White man who struggled with church culture as a child, didn't find answers to his questions in the church as much as in other communities, where the us/them dynamic was less prevalent. He says that as he engaged philosophy and religion both, "I realized that being mixed was exactly the theological journey I was on." As a Christian who also has a number of atheist friends, he says he's more comfortable with ambiguity than most White folks he knows, both religious and nonreligous. But it's been an arduous journey to learn to appreciate his place in the middle ground.

IS RESISTANCE FUTILE?

Pastor Efrem Smith writes, "As long as the church does not look like the place where we will live eternally, we should be uncomfortable . . . as long as the primary picture of the church in America is a segregated one, we should feel uncomfortable."[11] When it came to the growth of my identity in Christ, I needed a church where people weren't just willing to make the *other* comfortable but were also willing to be uncomfortable themselves—to feel discomforted even—in terms of ethnic and cultural norms.

I add *discomforted* here because being *uncomfortable* can be a mostly mental exercise, while being discomforted requires making the active choice of allowing oneself to be acted upon. It's one thing to be slightly uncomfortable but mostly still within your comfort zone, to passively welcome the *other* into your "home" without making any substantial changes. It's quite another thing to *choose* to sit in discomfort, to yield a sense of safety, consistency, and power; to allow others to rearrange the furniture and make themselves truly at home.

We multiethnic folks live in this tension every day, so there's something significant about majority-culture people going out of their way to be discomforted. When they're willing merely to be uncomfortable, they may want to make others feel comfortable, but they still remain within their majority-culture context. That's commendable, but it's only the beginning. When majority-culture folks are willing to be *discomforted*, they're willing to experience some small part of the pain and exhaustion of being a minority. To be discomforted, they must be willing to be acted upon and to admit that God is in control of his church. Then, and only then, can they begin to understand some of the weariness that comes from feeling like a constant outsider with no voice.

That's part of the gift we mixed people can bring to our spheres of influence: an understanding of that weariness, of the effects both negative and positive of being turned into the *other*. For most people of color, the constant silencing is harmful but, by God's grace, also formative. We know how to *listen*. A person in any minority situation may be silenced—in terms of ethnicity, gender, sexuality, socioeconomic status, and so on. But God can redeem and use the sinful actions of others to bring insight and healing.

And though it hurts, when we're quieted by the Lord through all sorts of circumstances, we can finally listen to him, not to the lies that fill our society, our churches, our families, and even our own heads.

EMBODIED SANCTIFICATION

The lesson many a person of color understands all too well is that of letting go of personal preferences and holding tight to what we know to be true in the Bible. This mentality is a must for all believers, and especially for us people of multiethnicity. And it's a way that we can instruct the church in growing in grace. When majority-culture folks are forced to figure out what the *essential* doctrines are,[12] to hold tightly to those, and to let go of the rest, that's a truly sanctifying event. Even more so, when they learn, through perseverance that becomes habit, how to be *willing* to submit themselves to that process, it shows they're willing to give up preferences and to embrace changes that are difficult—for the good of the *other*.

Then majority-culture folks can start the journey of understanding the helplessness of constantly having to give up one's own preferences. If White folks truly want to welcome the *other*, they must be willing to explore what parts of their own culture fall under biblical mandate and what parts are preferential only. Then they can understand some of the sadness that comes with constantly having to assimilate to the dominant culture.

And we multiethnic folks can show the way. When God's people are willing to embrace true solidarity with the "stranger who sojourns with [us]," to provide the protections and respect God has commanded to be shown to people, that is the gospel at work (Lev 19:34 ESV). Is there anything more biblical and central to the gospel than being willing to set aside our rights, privileges, and security for the good of the *other*—the way Jesus did (Phil 2:3-7)?

All humans are made in the image of God—the *imago Dei*. All of God's redeemed children are being made into the image of Christ, our elder brother. And, specifically, we multiethnic believers can have the privilege of joining Christ in showcasing some of the new-heavens and new-earth reconciliation that is to come (Rev 7:9). We mixed folks image Jesus by our unique genetic makeup—in our very bones. When it seems we don't belong anywhere else, we belong in the kingdom—not in spite of our multiethnicity but in celebration of it.

So it's truly heartbreaking when we mixed folks don't feel welcome in the physical manifestation of the kingdom—the church. When we hear that a group of believers is multiethnic but then discover that multiethnic *people* are ignored in that group, there's much to lament. In those situations, it's only the truth of the gospel and the promise of God's coming justice-shalom that bring us through.

When we enter a space that's very intentional in its multiethnicity but only for *monoethnic* majority and minority folks, it hurts. We're made to feel guilty when others' carefully constructed categories are blown apart by us simply walking through the door. When it comes time to have "ethnic-specific breakouts" to better honor people in their ethnicities, but multiethnic people aren't considered, that sends a message. Yes, it may be unintentional, but it also verifies that there are systemic practices and structures that need to be reevaluated, in light of Scripture, by leaders who may have grown too comfortable with the status quo.

A HEAVENLY CITIZENSHIP

As mentioned earlier, we are *all* people of multiple ethnicities, even White folks in America who benefit from majority-culture privilege and monoethnic folks who don't feel the same internal disconnect as we mixed folks do. Yes, heavenly citizenship is true for all of us who are not home yet. But for minorities—especially mixed-race folks—that citizenship can have extra precious significance.

The worldwide church body all-too-often doesn't showcase her heavenly citizenship. Instead of mirroring that Revelation 7:9 community with diversity of all types, humans tend to gather with people like them, who think, look, vote, and act like them. People tend to forget that our ultimate allegiance is to the kingdom of God, and we lose sight of longing for heaven.

Though this happens to us mixed folks as well, our ethnic makeup does help us see things in different ways. I'm not claiming that we always have our priorities straight, but out of our *weakness*, God shows himself strong. God reminds us that the church is bigger, more beautiful, and more diverse than we can even imagine. That's a gift we mixed folks can give to the church—a reminder that we aren't home yet, that there are still people on the outside looking in, that we still have work to do in ourselves and in our spheres of influence to see the "least of these" and to minister to them.

Pastor Smith quotes author Zenos E. Hawkinson's thoughts about the way that God brings growth out of hardship:

In my bones I feel that we are being uprooted now in a variety of ways, personally and communally. . . . Our forebears . . . found strange places and moments of unutterable anguish and loneliness [until] suddenly a voice says, "You are not alone. I have purposes. I have things to be done." . . . Our own tradition in the Covenant Church gives us reason to have confidence that people can be thrown bodily out of their accustomed culture and create new things as a consequence.[13]

As I continue to learn to praise God for my multiethnicity, I also learn to create new relationships and patterns, new ways of seeing others. In doing this, I can delight in the ways that other marginalized groups uniquely reflect the image of God. Appreciating my own story has allowed me to appreciate how the stories of others reflect the gospel: first parents, adoptees, adoptive families and parents of color;[14] refugees; the poor; the depressed and grieving; and believers in prison and in slavery (Eph 1:5; Mt 8:20; Ps 9:18; Ps 69:33). We mixed folks have many things we can showcase and teach the church when we're well-resourced, cared for, and listened to. So it's imperative that the church as an institution does the good work of seeing and loving people of multiethnicity.

When I first read *Check All That Apply*, I was blown away. Hearing for the first time that I could image Jesus *in all my complexity* was a beautiful, humbling, overwhelming, life-changing thing. It was truly transformative. Reading that book, finding a multiethnic church, having mixed friends and biologically mixed children, and other things, have enabled me to be on the journey of better learning to love my multi-ethnicity, to see it as a gift to myself and to the world. I'm learning not to apologize for my very existence and my category-defying presence, which makes everything complicated for "normal" people. I've begun to rejoice in being the person God designed me to be.

I've experienced moments when I understand what it means to be whole, what it means to have an integrated cultural identity that neither discounts some aspects nor smashes them all together into the *other* category at the expense of the uniqueness of each culture. Being entrusted with the stories of other mixed people and then endeavoring to share them with others has also been instrumental in my spiritual growth and walk with Christ as a mixed woman. Hearing others' stories can do the seemingly contradictory work of helping us to see how others are both very much like us and also wonderfully different. We multiethnic folks can appreciate seeming contradictions in a very special way, and we can share that joy with the people that God places in our lives.

HOME SWEET HOME

Nearly fifteen years after becoming a believer and being nurtured in my first church (as well as in other wonderful mono-ethnic churches), God brought our family to a multiethnic church in Jackson, Mississippi (of all places). While far from perfect, our church has been a place of deep healing. The first time I attended, I thought, *I've finally found my people group—a people group made up of others. No one looks exactly like me, but no one looks exactly like everyone else, either. So everyone looks different, like me.*

In this new place, I found something I didn't realize I was looking for—nor would I have thought was available, even if I'd dreamed of it. I saw mixed couples, families formed through adoption, international folks and multilingual folks, brothers and sisters who are multiethnic and multicultural, all in the same church. And this group wasn't brought together because of being on the same college campus or crosscultural affinity group that might explain away the diversity.

There was something else at work. I did see wonderful monoethnic people and families of several ethnicities, but when at its best and viewed as a whole, our church looked like me. It was the first time in my life that I could fit in completely, because no one completely fits in. Our commonalities center around the fact that unity and diversity not only can coexist but they actually are part of God's gracious plan. The gospel shows us how unity and diversity are integral to each other.

In this beautiful, broken city in the Deep South where so many horrible things have been done to people of color, I get emotional every time a White elder (from our multiracial elder board) serves Communion to our Black head pastor. In the very building where, as recently as the 1970s, Black Christians were turned away at the doors by White men in positions of power, now some small measure of shalom-justice is coming. As I see majority-culture people humbling themselves to serve—and to specifically serve minorities—I see a glimpse of how it will be when Jesus returns and reconciles everything. The choice that the pastoral search committee made fifteen years ago to pursue a Black head pastor showed their faithfulness in following Jesus and refusing to accept the status quo. They pressed on in search of the kingdom.

Though we mixed folks sometimes feel we don't have a home, we also have the beautiful ability to make a home wherever we go, out of necessity. Brandee loves that being biracially Black and White has given her "an ability to be anywhere and know that you belong." We people of multi-ethnicity can show the church how to live in the "here and not yet" liminal-space reality of our current church age and to rest in what we have, even as we long for something more. This is an important lesson for the church to learn: the reality of our future worship allows us to invite others into our current worship.

HEALTHY DISRUPTIONS TO UNHEALTHY PATTERNS

God can use a truly multiethnic and cultural experience to change hearts. I worried that it would be awkward when my mixed-couple parents came to visit us in Mississippi. But my dad, who was then not a believer in Christ, was amazed when he joined us for a church service. Like me, he had no category for a multiethnic church. As a Black man raised in the South, his experiences of segregation and abuse had gone hand in hand with his experiences of a divided, divisive church. But God spoke to him through his encounters with multiethnic groups of believers, worshiping and serving side by side, both in Mississippi and later in my hometown back in New Mexico. He became a believer shortly before his death, and I'm so grateful for how God brought healing to my dad's wounded heart through the diversity of his people.

I've realized that in truly diverse spaces, being multiethnic is a consequence—albeit an intentional one—of the gospel being properly preached. The gospel *is* the story of reconciliation, of sins being repented of and forgiven, of justice coming to bear on brokenness—the precious story of the Prince of Peace bringing his humble reconciliation to bear. As more recent political developments in our country have shown majority-culture folks just how deeply divided the country still is, it is becoming more clear how desperately we need true peace, true reconciliation, true unity.

And as we continue to reckon with the effects of a global pandemic, we see anew how broken the entirety of creation is. As we mixed folks know, being whole and healed in any sense can come only through the moving of the Holy Spirit—something no human can predict, easily categorize, or get "comfortable" and ready for. The shaking of our self-built identity is often one of the first ways Jesus gets our attention.

Like many of us mixed folks, I've been wrestling with these ideas for years. It's been a time of change and self-realization. I love our church dearly, but I'm realizing the limitations of calling it *multi*ethnic, when it's primarily a White-and-Black congregation, as well as the limitations of calling it multi-*cultural*, when it's primarily composed of folks who are all the same socioeconomically, educationally, and ecclesiastically.

I don't have answers for what to do when too many of us White people (and yes, I'm including myself here) show up and "ruin" everything. I'm not sure what to make of the large numbers of majority-culture folks who love the fact that the preacher gets excited, the choir sways, and the organ hums . . . but get upset if someone mentions police brutality or the plight of immigrants or the complexity of having our church building on lands stolen from the Choctaw.

In terms of my own preferences in styles of worship, I have to wonder this: though I feel strongly that majority-culture people must be willing to be discomforted, how often am I okay with being uncomfortable myself? Have I forgotten that in a truly multiethnic/cultural church, everyone will be uncomfortable to some degree? Have I made myself so comfortable that I've forgotten, as worship leader Sandra Maria Van Opstal reminds us, "in a multiethnic community no members should be made to feel like perpetual guests"[15]? I must continue to work against my idolization of what I think a multiethnic church should look like.

I must continue asking, how much do I expect the church to look *exactly* like me in its diversity and to make me feel at home? Have I lost sight of Jesus' call to take up my cross and follow him, to go out to the world and not take with me all the comforts of home? When it comes to matters of yielding power and comfort to others, where does my pale-skinned privilege meet my mixed-heritage grief?

These are questions that we people of multiethnicity ask ourselves often.

FIGHTING THE GOOD FIGHT

Therein lies both the joy and the pain—the reality of the mixed experience. To avoid the triumphalism of which author Soong-Chan Rah warns us, we need to keep in sight the brokenness, the disconnect, the discord that clings to us all. Even as we sing songs of joy and hope, we do so only in the context of singing songs of lament.[16] By nature of our experiences, we mixed folks have this built in. And as multiethnic churches continue to look more like the majority culture, all of us must ask why this is and what Jesus would have us do about it.

In recounting a particularly difficult moment of setback in the fight against injustice, Rah says, "Even after multiple laments had been offered, we couldn't just get over it. There was no 'manning up' and no *happy, idealized multiracial worship service to run to.* Lament was needed once again."[17] Van Opstal reminds the church that "we must be skilled at developing processes of change that help people embrace the discomfort."[18] We mixed folks are susceptible, as are all people, to losing sight of the various people groups in our church bodies. But one way in which multiethnic people are a unique gift to the church is how we have developed these processes of change and adaptation in our everyday lives.

We also have a strong understanding of the *other*. Due to our hyper-awareness of the various people groups reflected in our own individual bodies, we also tend to notice marginalized people groups, even (and perhaps especially) ones that aren't reflected in our ethnic makeup.

ANTICIPATING THE NEW HEAVENS AND THE NEW EARTH IN THE HERE AND NOW

Many of us multiethnic and multicultural believers can speak of our personal, lived experiences—if only the church will listen. Our viewpoints are important in understanding the need for multiethnic believers to have a broader voice in church settings. We deserve to be heard! We mixed folks have much to teach the church about contextualizing with grace and authenticity and about pursuing justice with humility and conviction. Lo, standing in the goodness of a multiethnic Native and White body, puts it beautifully: "Mixed people are kind of a mirror" which can reflect truth back to the world and magnify Christ's light to the nations.

The multiethnic and multicultural church is where we—all of his children—image God and his people. It's where we can be our true selves, proclaiming God's will and work as "good, pleasing and perfect" (Rom 12:2). And the worldwide multiethnic and multicultural church is where Emmanuel has chosen to continue his work of healing and growing all of us, in preparation for that blessed day when we will gather in the new heavens and the new earth.

Epilogue

Our Story

So let me ask the proverbial question, once again:
What are you?

Are you "half and half"?

One-sixteenth Choctaw? One-fourth Sioux?

Do you have one drop of African blood?

Are you "simply" Black? Persian? South Asian? Pacific Islander?

Or do you live in the hyphen of Asian-American?[1]

How do you embrace your *mestizaje* experience?

Are you Brown? Black? White? Beige?

Now let me rephrase the question: *Who has God made you to be?*

Our individual answers may be similar to one or more of the above, but when we frame the question through Jesus, we bring things back into their proper, healthy order. Both identities are important, but one is primary. Our ethnicity matters because Jesus is leading us in it. Our ethnicity is beautiful and purposeful because it reflects God and his kingdom. It doesn't get erased in the new creation; it flourishes in the new heavens

and the new earth. Our ethnicity isn't the most defining part
of us, but it points back to Christ. So maybe I'm really asking
this: Where are you from? Where are you going?

Or even better, where are *we* from and where are *we* going?
Let's reflect on our heritage; let's think about the "great cloud
of witnesses" (Heb 12:1) who await the inauguration of the
Revelation 7 "Beloved Community," a family peopled with
Christians from every tribe, tongue, and nation. Do we see
ourselves in that mighty throng? Can the larger church remember that, as a multiethnic group, there are people who
have multiple tribes, tongues, and nations within their embodied selves? By the grace and passion of the Holy Spirit, I
believe so.

So, what is a mixed Christian? What is a mixed blessing?
We mixed folks are blessings indeed to our families, the
church, and the world. We are each part of a new race of redeemed children, each of us a beautiful mixed blessing in the
body of Christ. And he is the diverse God-man who exists in
eternal love within the trinitarian unity of diversity. This new,
redeemed human race doesn't blot out or whitewash skin
color and other distinctives. Rather, these differences, which
God created for good, are highlighted and celebrated. Christ
speaks to, through, and on behalf of mixed people, for his
glory and for the good of his church. So hear this invitation,
siblings. Let's listen and rejoice that he created mixed
blessings such as ourselves to be a specific manifestation of
his goodness.

What a precious privilege we multiethnic folks have in our
calling to embody reconciliation in our very existence and to
call the church to do the same!

When we are in authentically multiethnic spaces, we know the privilege of being surrounded by a diversity that's biblical, authentic, and representative of our community— and of the church at large. This is something a monoethnic space in the world can never be. Do we see ourselves as those who have the privilege of surrounding others with our diversity? Even as we await our ultimate residency in that holy city that will not fade and doesn't need "the sun or moon to shine on it, for the glory of God gives it light" (Rev 21:23), we have been given a place to make camp and call home. God has called us to wait with anticipation for the New Jerusalem, to let our stranger-and-sojourner, mixed-blessing status drive us in mission.

Mixed people and those in intentionally mixed spaces understand the feeling of never quite being at home, but we also can make a home wherever we go. We can sit in the tension of the seemingly contradictory concept that this earth is not our final home but also that we have been brought here by the Lord. Even in our exile to Babylon, while we await the Lord's deliverance, we are called to "build houses and settle down, plant gardens and eat what they produce. . . . Also, seek the peace and prosperity of the city to which I have carried you into exile. Pray to the LORD for it, because if it prospers, you too will prosper" (Jer 29:5, 7).

All humans need to know they aren't alone. In conjunction with their Race Issue project, *National Geographic* created a video showing six different people being presented with pictures of complete strangers who shared a large portion of their genetic makeup and thus looked very similar.[2] When presented with the pictures, one man grew very emotional and was flustered by his own response. I have a guess as to why he grew weepy: he was feeling the shock and maybe even the hope of seeing other people who experienced the world the same way he did, due to their appearance. For some multi-ethnic folks, finding people who look like us can be a rare and overwhelming experience. It can also bring healing. But perhaps we all draw too narrow a definition of what "looking like us" means.

For those who are, like me, part of a crossculturally blended family, there's a unique aspect to our story, one that can be extremely difficult to quantify. And for those with albinism, vitiligo, and other specifically appearance-related characteristics, there are distinct issues that come into play. These siblings are also seen and welcomed at the table. We multiethnic people know some of their experiences, so let's corporately confess the ways in which we in the church haven't accepted—much less honored—the story of families who don't fit the majority-culture stereotype of what a healthy family looks like.

Here we see the crux of the mixed experience and what we have to offer the church: we mixed blessings are a testament to the healing and reconciliation that can and does exist within God's family. We don't have to measure the stories of physically displaced refugees against the stories of emotionally displaced mixed folks. Nor do we have to pit the stories of how differently abled people experience discrimination against the stories of how we mixed folks experience discrimination. All our stories deserve their own places of honor: spaces where they are listened to and lamented. All of our stories have some points of similarity that can be used to help build bridges between people and between different families. When we in the church are doing our God-given job and making space for lament and for empowering the weak and the wounded, displacement narratives and discrimination experiences of all kinds form a rich narrative of God's faithfulness in our hardships.

As I talked with various people, I discovered I'm not the only one who has felt trapped in the hallway when it's time to divide into ethnic groups. Kaylyn, who is a Korean American transracial adoptee, shared her experience of facing a dilemma similar to mine and of being mentored by an honored "auntie" within the Asian community. As Kaylyn stood there sniffling and wondering what to do, Auntie Lisa told her something that has stuck with her, even several years later: "Yes, you don't belong, and that's okay." Lisa said. "If the hallway is your home, just decorate it! Here you have access to all the rooms; you can come and go. It's okay if that's where you are."

Picture it, siblings. Transforming that beige hallway with an intricate rug from the Middle East flowing down the center. Finding comfortable chairs to place along the sides, embroidered with bright Native designs and delicate beading. Hanging pictures of different countries, different families, different faces along the walls. Bringing in fresh fruits from Asian countries, bright flowers from the United States and all over Europe, sweet delicacies from Latin countries and all across the continent of Africa. This is a space that shows us a glimmer of what the new heavens and earth will be like.

Listen—the sound of drumming fills the air. Hear the shimmering tinkle of chimes, the rhythmic clapping of hands raised in joy, and the soothing rumble of the organ. Can you hear it? Soak up the sounds of an eternal harmony of voices all raised in their own languages, yet speaking and singing as one.

Sure, it gets crowded sometimes. We may choose to retreat to one room or another. We may decide to hide on an entirely different floor. We might decorate our hallway only one way, even as we acknowledge the complexity of all our ethnic heritages. We may redecorate often, or never. We may find ourselves with lots of company, or sitting alone.

Except for one sure fixture, which will never change, and truly never leave us alone. Because look there, on the throne—there sits the risen Lord Jesus, at the right hand of the Father, the ultimate mixed blessing for his people. This in-between space is our home because *he* is our home. And he's welcoming us, with open, nail-pierced hands. We will sing with him and to him, forever, and we can start now.

This is *our* story; this is *his* story. Let us tell it together, fellow beloved-of-God mixed blessings. Hallelujah!

Where I'm From

Chandra Crane

I am from sandwich cookies.
From half-chocolate,
half-vanilla Oreos,
black, white, yellow
   and delicious

I am from the Land of Enchantment
Spicy sweet New Mexico green chile
roasting in 50 gallon drums
outside weather-faded grocery stores,
aroma drifting all across town

I am from the Peach State,
the Magnolia State
    "Strange fruit" and hubcap-sized blossoms
  strange customs and mandated politeness
delicious, beautiful, welcoming
juicy and irresistible.

I'm from *sawasdee ka* (hello, goodbye),
mai pen rai (means nevermind), and
sanuk (because the Land of Smiles)
From Wisnu Ampawasiri and Victoria Wood.

I'm from the New Mexican spirit of *de nada* (no problem,
    it was nothing),
mi casa es su casa (what's mine is yours),
and side-splitting laughter

  from "Pull yourself up by your own bootstraps"
  and "What would the neighbors think?"
  from secrets, shame, servitude
  and self-security

I'm from folk music hymn-sings,
white dudes rapping,
Motown and swaying gospel choirs,
orange-clad monks chanting.

I'm from the High Plains of New Mexico and
the lush greenery of Thailand,
from potlucks and feasts—
whether *huevos rancheros,*
"potted chicken" falling-off-the-bones tender,
or spicy *kiew* curry,
rice with everything.

And also, somehow, from Roger and Victoria Garrett,
from the African tribe that my dad swore came over
        to America *by train*

and yet
from the Asian culture who points and laughs to defuse
awkward situations
who uses pungent *nam pla* instead of table salt.

   I am from all the people who are in desperate need of
        gospel truth.

In dusty storage boxes with baby clothes and faded pictures,
is my heritage, all jumbled together.

I am from multiethnicity.
I am a
walking
   cultural
        appreciation . . .

I am mixed.
   I am blessed.[3]

Acknowledgments

I AM SO GRATEFUL FOR:

Al Hsu, my amazing editor, who guided me through many a self-inflicted storm and curbed my wordiness (but can't be held responsible for the length of this particular section).

All the IVP staff: especially Tiffany, Maila, Christina, Krista, Justin Paul, Anna, Helen, Lorraine, Kathryn, Andrew, Lori, Allie, Tara, Kari, David and the distribution team, Cindy, Ellen, Ethan, Audrey, Rebecca, Paloma, Elissa, and David and the design wizards.

My fantastic launch team and thoughtful endorsers.

Erin Fults of Acorn Studio, for an amazing photo shoot to showcase me as a new author.

Jemar Tisby, for taking your experiences in multicultural circles to write a gracious, powerful foreword, and for your even more gracious friendship.

Jen Hollingsworth, for your amazing work with the Four Postures model.

Julie Ruark of 5B Creative, for a classy website, empowerment and mentoring galore, and infinite patience.

Beth and Byron Borger of Hearts & Minds Books, for keeping me supplied with good books and great conversations.

Bethany Horvath, for helping me get organized and magnifying my voice with your amazing consulting talents.

My biological and legal fam: K, A, & E (my three faves), Grams & Gramps, all the Ampawasiris, Gran & Granpa, the Hwangs, the Garrett-Starnes-McFaddens, the Flint-Rices, Aunt J, the Lewises, and all the Crane crew.

All who shared their thoughts and stories (this is *our* book), especially folks who took the time for interviews: Niki, Brennan, Steve, Melody, Sherrene, Kristina, Brandee, Kaylyn, Aton, Cheryl, Bethany, Kylene, Lo, Tiffany, York, Karen, Kevin, Adam, Morgan, Sundee, and Bekah; and of course, King Jesus, whose multi*everything* story gives meaning to all others.

Writing Workshop 2017 peeps: Al, Lisa, Bethany, Rebecca, Paula Frances, Natalia, John, Kathy, Sean, and Brenda.

And other IV fam, past and present: AAM & BCM; the SEAM team & crew; the Multiethnic Initiatives team; GFM Red River & ATL team; IV Gulf & River; the Mixed Advisory Team & Mixed Staff fam; HeadStrong fam; IV Mamas; Adoptees fam; That Other Group sibs; and especially Megan, Andy, Vince, Kristen, the Changs, Sabrina, Tim, the Clarks, Kirsten, Beth, Jeremy, Christina Marie, Maureen, Steve, Tom, and Hannah.

These fierce, supportive women: Latasha, Emily, Audra, Jess, B, Steph, Brenna, Andra, Anna, Kdids, Erin, Christy, Jen, Keren, and Carolyn.

Our MS/ATL community, especially: Smiley, the Whites, Donny & Samuel, the Hubbards, Janet, Marcelene, all the Redeemer, ChristChurch, and WMBC small group fams (past, present, and future), the Silvers, the SA&E crew, Coalesce folks, and errybody who's dined at our table.

MC folks, especially: Tiffany, Ky'sha, Jhasmine, KeNosha, Ashley, Otis, Dean Wendy, and the Friday L.A.W. Fellowship.

Our NM fam, especially: Danny, Tasha, Betty & Co., the Jileks, Joyce, Len, the Goolsbys, Nico, Becky, Chris, the Reeveses, Mosaic Church fam, and previous creative/writing teachers: Mrs. Sikes, Mrs. Stratton, Ms. Thompson Hasenmueller, Mrs. Rippee, Dr. Williamson, and Dr. Caldwell.

And my online peeps who have highlighted my voice and encouraged me, especially: Katclyn, Gabriel, the Reynoldses, the Welchers, Paige, Jenna, Claire, Kristin, JJ, Joy, Esau, Allie, Dorothy, Marlena, Timothy, the Brookses, April, Sarah, Brandon, #WeirdEvaTwit/wct, The Clutch, all the Entrusted Women, and the good folks at Dordt University's iAt.

Appendix A

Recommended Reading

RACIAL RECONCILIATION—NONFICTION

Michael O. Emerson and Christian Smith, *Divided by Faith: Evangelical Religion and the Problem of Race in America* (New York: Oxford University Press, 2001).

Charles Marsh and John M. Perkins, *Welcoming Justice: God's Movement Toward Beloved Community* (Downers Grove, IL: InterVarsity Press, 2018).

Sandhya Rani Jha, *Pre-Post-Racial America: Spiritual Stories from the Front Lines* (Nashville, TN: Chalice Press, 2015).

Sarah Shin, *Beyond Colorblind: Redeeming Our Ethnic Journey* (Downers Grove, IL: InterVarsity Press, 2017).

Jemar Tisby, *The Color of Compromise: The Truth About the American Church's Complicity in Racism* (Grand Rapids, MI: Zondervan, 2019).

MIXED PERSPECTIVE—NONFICTION

Brian Bantum, *Redeeming Mulatto: A Theology of Race and Christian Hybridity* (Waco, TX: Baylor University Press, 2016).

Sundee Tucker Frazier, *Check All That Apply: Finding Wholeness as a Multiracial Person* (Downers Grove, IL: InterVarsity Press, 2002).

MIXED PERSPECTIVE—MEMOIR/FICTION

Zinzi Clemmons, *What We Lose* (New York: Viking, 2017).

Sharon M. Draper, *Blended* (New York: Atheneum/Caitlyn Dlouhy Books, 2018).

Sundee T. Frazier, *The Other Half of My Heart* (New York: Yearling, 2011) and several other young adult novels.

Andrew Garrod, Robert Kilkenny, and Christina Gomez, eds., *Mixed: Multiracial College Students Tell Their Life Stories* (Ithaca, NY: Cornell University Press, 2013).

Adib Khorram, *Darius the Great is Not Okay* (New York: Penguin Books, 2018).

James McBride, *The Color of Water: A Black Man's Tribute to His White Mother* (New York: Riverhead Books, 2006).

Stephen Murphy-Shigematsu, *When Half Is Whole: Multiethnic Asian American Identities* (Stanford, CA: Stanford University Press, 2012).

Trevor Noah, *Born a Crime: Stories from a South African Childhood* (New York: One World, 2019).

Chandra Prasad, ed., *Mixed: An Anthology of Short Fiction on the Multiracial Experience* (New York: W. W. Norton & Company, 2016).

Cindy Wilson, *Too Much Soul: The Journey of an Asian Southern Belle* (Atlanta: Too Much Soul, 2018).

Appendix B

Parenting Guide

Questions for Monoethnic Parents to Ask Themselves:

- What do I know about my own cultural heritage? What do I want to teach my child(ren) about that part of their mixed heritage?

- What do I know about the other parts of my child(ren)'s ethnicity? What things do I need to educate myself about to be a good resource to them? What things are outside my ability to teach them? Where do I need to educate myself further, and where do I need to call in "aunties and uncles" to help my children learn about themselves?

- What issues of racism, prejudice, colorism, and favoritism do I have that I need to address? What would God have me do to work through these?

- How can I repent of my own sinful tendencies in private, so as not to make my child(ren) work through it with me, but also in transparency with them, so that my own struggles can be helpful to them?

Questions to Ask Mixed Children:

- What parts of your face look like (a relative)? Which parts remind you of (another relative)? How do you feel about that?

- Have people commented on your appearance? What did they ask you? Did it make you feel different emotions?

- What parts of your heritage would you like to learn about next?

- What does it mean to you to be multiethnic?

- What questions do you have about being mixed? Would you like to share your feelings?

- Did you know that Jesus is mixed? Can we read about that together? How do you think Jesus felt about his multiethnic family?

Resources/Exercises:

- The "Where I'm From" poem project—a template for writing a poem about family and identity. Be sure to allow your child(ren) to customize their poems as much as they'd like, with as many different parts as they'd like, to ensure that they are able to express the complexity of their mixed experience. Modeled after "Where I'm From" by George Ella Lyon (www.sausd.us/cms/lib /CA01000471/Centricity/Domain/3043/I%20Am %20From%20Poem.pdf); see also the original project and recent iterations at iamfromproject.com/resources.

- The "Hapa Project"—take a picture of your child(ren) and have them write their descriptors (ethnicity, interests, etc.) at the bottom of the picture. This project is great for a group of mixed kids. See the work of Kip Fulbeck for more information (www.kipfulbeck.com /the-hapa-project).

Study Guide

CHAPTER 1: MULTIETHNICITY 101

1. What interactions have you had regarding your appearance? Are they mostly positive, negative, or a combination of the two?

2. Do you like sharing your ethnic identity story? How do you set boundaries with people who ask about your ethnicity?

3. How do you define *race, ethnicity,* and *multiethnic?* Do you use the term *mixed,* or do you prefer another word?

4. Do you identify with the two descriptors (diversity within family and diversity based on others' expectations)? Either of them, one of them, or neither of them? Do you have other ways to explain your mixed experience?

5. Do you relate to any groups who are multicultural without being multiethnic—multiethnic/blended families, transracial adoptees, etc.? How can we, as a community of mixed folks, help build bridges?

CHAPTER 2: MULTIETHNICITY 102

1. Do you see yourself represented in media, entertainment, and politics? If so, how do you feel when you do? If not, how does that affect your identity?

2. Do you resonate with the ideas of *intersectionality*? Do you feel these issues mostly in your multiracial experience, or also in terms of gender, sexual orientation, physical ability, socioeconomic status, etc.?

3. Where do you feel sadness in your ethnicity? Where do you feel joy? Do you ever feel weary?

4. Do you identify with the idea of *code-switching*? Is this something that is a large part of your life, or not as much? Do you think it's a positive or negative thing?

5. Does lamenting feel natural to you? Challenging or maybe scary? Does it feel unnecessary? How can we mixed folks engage the brokenness of this world, and how can our multiethnicity inform our approaches?

CHAPTER 3: REJECTING STEREOTYPES, UNDERSTANDING PROTOTYPES, EMBRACING STORIES

1. What stereotypes have been used against you? What stereotypes have you found yourself guilty of using? What strategies are there to identify and work through bias against others?

2. What prototypes do you see in your various ethnicities? Which ones do you see in yourself? Are there prototypes of you that you wish you understood better, or that other folks understood about you?

3. Does walking the line between cultural *appropriation* and cultural *appreciation* feel tiring to you? How can you rest well in God without losing sight of others' needs?

4. What parts of your cultural heritage do you feel most comfortable with? Are there parts that feel uncomfortable, off-limits, or completely foreign?

5. How can we mixed folks partner with each other to do the good work of identifying the parts of our cultures that are good, biblical, and instructive?

CHAPTER 4: MIXED FOLKS

1. How have you encountered colorism? How does colorism play into appreciating your skin tone? What parts of your appearance do you find positive, and which parts feel frustrating or negative?

2. Do you feel lonely in your mixed identity? If you have siblings, how has that helped, or hurt, your sense of belonging? Where do you go to find your "people?"

3. In what ways have monoethnic folks made you feel less than valuable, appropriate, or wanted? In what ways have they made you feel welcome?

4. Have you experienced a *"Where do I go?"* moment? What did you do?

5. How can we mixed folks be a good community to each other? What can we do to advocate for ourselves and others?

CHAPTER 5: MIXED IDENTITY IN
THE MULTIETHNIC CHRIST

1. What phrases/ideas in the church have been hurtful to you in your identity development? Helpful?

2. How does the multiethnic lineage of Christ make you feel? What parts of his identity feel inclusive to you? Are there parts that make you feel alienated? What would he have you learn from the complexities of his identity?

3. What parts of your mixed identity feel helpful to learning more about Jesus and his world? What parts feel difficult?

4. Can you identify with biblical heroes such as the Bleeding Woman, Esther, Timothy, Moses, Ruth, and Rahab? What other biblical and/or historical figures are an encouragement to you in your multiethnicity?

5. What does it mean that we are disrupters of people's expectations? How can we mirror Jesus in this way?

CHAPTER 6: EXPLORING AND
NURTURING MIXED IDENTITY

1. Do you feel this "here and not yet" tension? What parts of your identity connect to that? Ethnicity, gender, socioeconomics, etc.? In what ways do your experiences in this fallen world make you long for the new heavens and new earth?

2. The first part of the Multiethnic Identity Cycle is "Pray About Ethnic Formation." Does this part of the cycle feel

easier or harder than the others? What more do you want to learn about spiritual disciplines and prayer?

3. In part two, "Explore Our Ethnic Identity," there are a few suggestions on how and where to learn about our various heritages. Have you talked to family, researched ancestors, or traveled to learn more? What did you learn?

4. A main aspect of part two is also the Four Postures model. Which posture(s) do you relate to the most (solidarity, shifting, substitute, or singular)? How do you feel about postures that you don't identify with? Can you think of more postures that you occupy?

5. Part three is "Apply Truths to the Christian Walk." How can we do this in community? Does finding rest seem contradictory with working through our identities? How can we help each other feel loved and lovely?

CHAPTER 7: MIXED IDENTITY IN OUR FAMILIES AND COMMUNITIES

1. In what ways have you experienced safety and healing in your family? How have you experienced trauma? Where have you found healthy places for connecting with others?

2. How do you relate to your closest family members in terms of your multiethnicity? How do you relate to extended family? Do you feel appreciated, or shunned, or something else?

3. What traditions have been passed down to you? What traditions are you hoping to pass down to the

next generation of children, cousins, nieces and nephews, etc.?

4. What lies have you been told about your value and multiethnicity? What allies do you have to speak truth to you?

5. So what *is* a family, then? How can we foster healthy families and strong communities to make sure that mixed folks are resourced and loved well?

CHAPTER 8: MIXED IDENTITY IN THE CHURCH AND SOCIETY

1. How do you feel about monoethnic churches? If you're in a monoethnic church, what is the primary culture? If you're in a multiethnic church, does it seem as diverse as the website might advertise?

2. How do you discern whether a church's cultural practices are just a preference, or a matter of doctrine?

3. How do you see the dynamic between church culture and society at large? Do you think it's a healthy or unhealthy relationship? What would you like to see changed?

4. How much of your multiethnic heritage comes from joy, and how much from trauma? Which stories of your ancestors make you rejoice in your mixed story, and which ones make you lament?

5. How can we mixed folks support, teach, and convict our churches toward repentance and action? How can we do this while maintaining healthy boundaries and caring for ourselves well?

Notes

INTRODUCTION: WHAT ARE YOU?

[1]The term "Beloved Community" was first coined by Josiah Royce and popularized by Reverend Martin Luther King Jr. See "The King Philosophy," www
.thekingcenter.org/king-philosophy. See also Efrem Smith, *The Post-Black and Post-White Church: Becoming the Beloved Community in a Multi-Ethnic World* (San Francisco: Jossey-Bass, 2012), 5, electronic edition.

[2]Sundee Tucker Frazier, *Check All That Apply: Finding Wholeness as a Multiracial Person* (Downers Grove, IL: InterVarsity Press, 2002).

[3]There has been recent pushback against the term "racial reconciliation," with very compelling reasons. I fully support those who use other terms, even as I choose to continue to use the word "reconciliation." For me, it points toward Christ as our reconciler with both God and with other people. There was Edenic harmony before sin, and despite the distortions of colorism and racism, there will be perfect reconciliation again, in the new heavens and earth.

[4]Frazier, *Check All That Apply*, 130–31, 139.

[5]See Neil Rendall, *Moses, God's Tri-Cultural Man*, InterVarsity Christian Fellowship/USA Multiethnic Ministries Bible study, updated March 11, 2013, http://mem.intervarsity.org/sites/mem/files/Moses%20A%20Tricultural%20Man%20Bible%20Study%201%20-%20Ex%201-4_0.pdf, 4, accessed October 29, 2019.

[6]C. S. Lewis, *The Weight of Glory and Other Addresses* (New York: Harper One, 1949), 246, electronic edition.

1 MULTIETHNICITY 101: THE FOUNDATION OF BEING MIXED

[1]Ta-Nehisi Coates, "What We Mean When We Say 'Race is a Social Construct,'" *The Atlantic*, May 15 2013, www.theatlantic.com/national/archive/2013/05/what-we-mean-when-we-say-race-is-a-social-construct/275872.

²Megan Gannon, "Race is a Social Construct, Scientists Argue," Scientific American, 2016, www.scientificamerican.com/article/race-is-a-social-construct -scientists-argue/.

³Jemar Tisby, *The Color of Compromise: The Truth about the American Church's Complicity in Racism* (Grand Rapids, MI: Zondervan, 2019), 26.

⁴Ta-Nehisi Coates, "What We Mean."

⁵Ana Gonzalez-Barrera and Mark Hugo Lopez, "Is being Hispanic a matter of race, ethnicity or both?," June 15, 2015, www.pewresearch.org/fact -tank/2015/06/15/is-being-hispanic-a-matter-of-race-ethnicity-or-both/.

⁶The term Hispanic has fallen out of favor due to its implications of Spanish conquest. However it's still preferred by many in the Southwestern United States, along with Chicano/a.

⁷United States Census Bureau, "Why We Ask Questions about . . . Hispanic or Latino Origin," www.census.gov/acs/www/about/why-we-ask-each-question /ethnicity/.

⁸While still used by some, Caucasian has also fallen out of use, due to there being an actual Caucasus region in Eastern Europe. White folks in the United States often refer to themselves as "European American," which also has its downsides. Europe, as a region, has many countries where pale skin is not the norm; and especially with globalization and immigration, a European can be of any skin tone. However, I often use Caucasian or European in referring to the immigration waves of previous centuries.

⁹See Andy Crouch, *Culture Making: Recovering Our Creative Calling* (Downers Grove, IL: InterVarsity Press, 2008).

¹⁰In the United States, "colored" was first applied to Black folks and emphasized being nonwhite. In South Africa, interestingly enough, "coloured" was applied to mixed folks and was criminalized. In the United States, mixed marriages were illegal; in South Africa, mixed children were illegal. See Trevor Noah's autobiography, *Born a Crime* (Penguin Random House: New York, 2019).

¹¹"People of Color," abbreviated as POC, is a generally positive catchall for non-white folks. After many years of use by some, it became more popular in the 1960s, and by the late 1980s it had been embraced by minorities as a positive way to describe themselves and their experiences (both good and bad). See William Safire, "ON LANGUAGE: People of Color," November 20, 1998, www .nytimes.com/1988/11/20/magazine/on-language-people-of-color.html.

¹²Efrem Smith, *The Post-Black and Post-White Church: Becoming the Beloved Community in a Multi-Ethnic World* (San Francisco: Jossey-Bass, 2012), electronic edition, 83, 85.

[13]Sundee Tucker Frazier, *Check All That Apply: Finding Wholeness as a Multiracial Person* (Downers Grove, IL: InterVarsity Press, 2002), 170-71.

[14]Akemi Johnson, "Who Gets To Be 'Hapa'?" Code Switch, National Public Radio, August 8, 2016, www.npr.org/sections/codeswitch/2016/08/08 /487821049/who-gets-to-be-hapa.

[15]Interestingly, a few of the mixed Asian and White folks I talked to said that they were amazed to visit Hawai'i and experience a strong sense of belonging because being mixed and looking part Asian is the norm there.

[16]See the works of authors such as Gloria Anzaldúa, Josue David Cisneros, and Nichole Margarita Garcia, "'We Didn't Cross The Border, The Border Crossed Us:' The Importance Of Ethnic Studies," Diverse: Issues In Higher Education, July 16, 2019, www.diverseeducation.com/article/148729.

[17]D'Vera Cohn, "It's official: Minority babies are the majority among the nation's infants, but only just," Pew Research Center, June 23, 2016, www.pewresearch .org/fact-tank/2016/06/23/its-official-minority-babies-are-the-majority -among-the-nations-infants-but-only-just/.

[18]Kim Parker, et al., "Multiracial in America: Proud, Diverse and Growing in Numbers," Pew Research Center, June 11, 2015, www.pewsocialtrends .org/2015/06/11/multiracial-in-america/.

[19]Robin DiAngelo, *White Fragility: Why It's So Hard for White People to Talk About Racism* (Boston: Beacon Press, 2018), xv.

[20]All interview quotations as well as quotations from survey responses were gathered by the author throughout 2018 and 2019, and are cited with permission of the participants, some with a pseudonym.

[21]Frazier, *Check All That Apply*, 162-63.

[22]Randy Woodley, *Living in Color: Embracing God's Passion for Ethnic Diversity* (Downers Grove, IL: InterVarsity Press, 2004), 108.

[23]Elizabeth Sung, "Race and Ethnicity Discourse and the Christian Doctrine of Humanity: a Systematic Sociological and Theological Appraisal," (PhD diss., Trinity International University, 2011), 209. ProQuest.

[24]Sarah Shin, *Beyond Colorblind: Redeeming Our Ethnic Journey* (Downers Grove, IL: InterVarsity Press, 2017), 6.

[25]Ben Lillie, "Be color brave, not color blind: Mellody Hobson speaks at TED2014," TED Blog, March 20, 2014, www.blog.ted.com/be-color-brave -not-color-blind-mellody-hobson-at-ted2014/.

[26]Interestingly, Jason Momoa, who is native Hawai'ian and mixed European Native American, has now had children with Lisa Bonet. So these step-siblings of Zoë Kravitz have their own unique multiethnicity.

[27]TIME, "Mixed-race Celebrities on Race, in Their Own Words," February 15, 2011, www.healthland.time.com/2011/02/15/mixed-race-celebrities-in-their-own-words/.

[28]The one-drop rule stated that if someone had any Black ancestors, they were Black—and therefore subject to slavery, Jim Crow laws, etc. See F. James Davis, Who is Black? One Nation's Definition (University Park: Penn State University Press, 1991), as quoted by Public Broadcasting Service, Frontline, www.pbs.org/wgbh/pages/frontline/shows/jefferson/mixed/onedrop.html.

[29]Michel Martin, "Actress Chloe Bennet Wants To Change The Narrative For Asian-Americans In Hollywood," *All Things Considered*, National Public Radio, September 3, 2017, www.npr.org/2017/09/03/548296823/actress-chloe-bennet-wants-to-change-the-narrative-for-asian-americans-in-hollyw. Actor James Roday initially chose his stage name because his surname, Rodriguez, was also limiting his casting options. Decades later, now an established actor (and in the current season of racial justice movements), he has chosen to reclaim his last name to honor his dad and stand with other Latinos (Michael Ausiello, "James Roday Details 'Deeply Personal' Decision to Reclaim Birth Name Rodriguez : 'I Want to Be the Most Honest Ally for My Community,'" TV Line, July 14, 2020, tvline.com/2020/07/14/james-roday-rodriguez-name-change-psych-2). Both he and Bennet have been told that they didn't look 'White enough' for the main character, nor 'Mexican' or 'Chinese' enough to fulfill diversity requirements and play the villain or sidekick.

[30]Smith, *The Post-Black*, 124.

[31]Smith, *The Post-Black*, 124-25.

[32]Maria P. P. Root, *The Multiracial Experience: Racial Borders as the New Frontier* (Thousand Oaks, CA: Sage Publications, 1996), 7.

2 MULTIETHNICITY 102: THE STORY OF BEING MIXED

[1]Excerpt from Thanhha Lai, "Black and White and Yellow and Red," *Inside Out & Back Again* (New York: HarperCollins, 2011).

[2]See Kimberlé Crenshaw, *On Intersectionality: The Essential Writings* (New York: The New Press, 2015), and Patricia Hill Collins and Sirma Bilge, *Intersectionality* (Malden, MA: Polity Press, 2016).

[3]Ana Gonzalez-Barrera and Mark Hugo Lopez, "Is Being Hispanic a Matter of Race, Ethnicity, or Both," Pew Research Center, June 15, 2015, www.pewresearch.org/fact-tank/2015/06/15/is-being-hispanic-a-matter-of-race-ethnicity-or-both/.

[4]Ana Gonzalez-Barrera , "'Mestizo' and 'mulatto': Mixed-race identities among U.S. Hispanics," Pew Research Center, July 10, 2015, www.pewresearch.org /fact-tank/2015/07/10/mestizo-and-mulatto-mixed-race-identities-unique -to-hispanics/.

[5]From the old, children's Sunday school song taught in many majority-culture churches.

[6]Arne Roets and Alain Van Hiel, as reviewed in "Research States that Prejudice Comes from a Basic Human Need and Way of Thinking" Association for Psychological Science, 2011, www.psychologicalscience.org/news/releases /research-states-that-prejudice-comes-from-a-basic-human-need-and-way -of-thinking.html.

[7]Encyclopaedia Britannica, s.v. "code-switching," www.britannica.com/topic /code-switching, accessed May 9, 2020.

[8]Cambridge Dictionary, s.v. "code-switching," www.dictionary.cambridge.org /us/dictionary/english/cultural-appropriation, accessed May 19, 2020.

[9]Soong-Chan Rah, *Prophetic Lament: A Call for Justice in Troubled Times* (Downers Grove, IL: InterVarsity Press, 2015), 22.

[10]Rah, *Prophetic Lament*, 23.

3 REJECTING STEREOTYPES, UNDERSTANDING PROTOTYPES, EMBRACING STORIES

[1]Chimamanda Ngozi Adichie, "The Danger of a Single Story," TED Talk, 2009, 10:12 and 10:52–11:55, www.ted.com/talks/chimamanda_ngozi_adichie _the_danger_of_a_single_story/transcript.

[2]Christena Cleveland, *Disunity in Christ: Uncovering the Hidden Forces That Keep Us Apart* (Downers Grove, IL: InterVarsity Press, 2013), 46-49.

[3]See Phillip Atiba Goff, et al., "The Essence of Innocence: Consequences of Dehumanizing Black Children," *Journal of Personality and Social Psychology*, 2014, 106:4, 526-45, accessible at www.apa.org/pubs/journals/rclcases/psp -a0035663.pdf; and Rebecca Epstein, Jamilia J. Blake, and Thalia González, "Girlhood Interrupted: The Erasure of Black Girls' Childhood," The Center on Poverty and Inequality, Georgetown Law, 2017, www.law.georgetown.edu /poverty-inequality-center/wp-content/uploads/sites/14/2017/08/girlhood -interrupted.pdf.

[4]See Ibram X. Kendi, *How to Be an Antiracist* (New York: One World, 2019).

[5]See Kat Chow, "'Model Minority' Myth Again Used As A Racial Wedge Between Asians and Blacks," Code Switch, National Public Radio, April 19, 2017, www.npr.org/sections/codeswitch/2017/04/19/524571669/model-minority-myth-again-used-as-a-racial-wedge-between-asians-and-blacks.

[6]Melodie J. Fox, "Prototype Theory: An Alternative Concept Theory for Categorizing Sex and Gender?," *Knowledge Organization* 38, 2011, 328.

[7]Online Etymology Dictionary, s.v. "stereotype" (στερεος), www.etymonline.com/word/stereotype.

[8]Online Etymology Dictionary, s.v. "prototype" (πρωτοτυπον/ς), www.etymonline.com/word/prototype.

[9]Stephen Murphy-Shigematsu, *When Half Is Whole: Multiethnic Asian American Identities* (Stanford, CA: Stanford University Press, 2012), 52.

[10]See Steven F. Riley commentary on "Tragic Mulatto/Mulatta," Mixed Race Studies, www.mixedracestudies.org/?p=454.

[11]Brian Bantum, *Redeeming Mulatto: A Theology of Race and Christian Hybridity* (Waco, TX: Baylor University Press, 2010), 111-12.

[12]Some of this section was originally published by Chandra Crane, "Honoring a Culture: Distinguishing Between Appropriation and Appreciation," *The Well*, October 24, 2019, thewell.intervarsity.org/focus/honoring-culture-distinguishing-between-appropriation-and-appreciation.

[13]Kat Chow, interview with Elizabeth Rule, "So What Exactly is 'Blood Quantum'?," Code Switch, National Public Radio, February 9, 2018, www.npr.org/sections/codeswitch/2018/02/09/583987261/so-what-exactly-is-blood-quantum.

[14]Alexandros Orphanides, "Why Mixed-Race Americans Will Not Save The Country," Code Switch, National Public Radio, March 8, 21017, www.npr.org/sections/codeswitch/2017/03/08/519010491/why-mixed-race-americans-will-not-save-the-country.

[15]Alexandros Orphanides, "Why Mixed-Race Americans."

[16]Adichie, "The Danger of a Single Story," 2009.

4 MIXED FOLKS: MINORITIES OF MINORITIES

[1]Clint Smith III, "Passed Down," *Counting Descent*, (Los Angeles: Write Bloody Publishing, 2016).

[2]Modified from Sundee Tucker Frazier, *Check All That Apply: Finding Wholeness as a Multiracial Person* (Downers Grove, IL: InterVarsity Press, 2002), 101.

[3]Sarah Shin, *Beyond Colorblind: Redeeming Our Ethnic Journey* (Downers Grove, IL: InterVarsity Press, 2017), 46.

[4]Nina Martin, "Lost Mothers: Nothing Protects Black Women from Dying in Pregnancy and Childbirth," ProPublica, in conjunction with National Public Radio, December 7, 2017, www.propublica.org/article/nothing-protects-black -women-from-dying-in-pregnancy-and-childbirth.

[5]Jemar Tisby, *The Color of Compromise: The Truth about the American Church's Complicity in Racism* (Grand Rapids: Zondervan, 2019), 16, 21.

[6]Leah Donnella, "'Racial Impostor Syndrome': Here Are Your Stories," Code Switch, National Public Radio, June 8, 2017, www.npr.org/sections /codeswitch/2017/06/08/462395722/racial-impostor-syndrome-here-are -your-stories.

[7]Keith and Gladys Hunt, *For Christ and the University: The Story of InterVarsity Christian Fellowship of the U.S.A., 1940-1990* (Downers Grove, IL: InterVarsity Press, 1991).

[8]The current minority ministries in our organization are Black Campus Ministries, Asian American Ministries, LaFe (Latino Fellowship), and Native InterVarsity (which hadn't been established then). As of this writing, we do not have a category for ministry to Middle Eastern staff, students, and faculty. We also do not have a department dedicated to ministering to mixed folks.

[9]I'm not denying that monoethnic minorities know the difficulty and exhaustion of code-switching that's required to survive in the dominant culture. But we mixed folks are in a unique situation: we are simultaneously part of both the minority and the majority culture (or two minority cultures with power differentials) in our very genes and/or family of origin. We have an internal struggle because choosing different cultural norms feels like accepting—or rejecting—part of ourselves, not just rejecting an outside entity.

[10]Frazier, *Check All That Apply*, 54-55.

5 MIXED IDENTITY IN THE MULTIETHNIC CHRIST

[1]The implications of this are many, in terms of how we have interpreted the Old Testament requirements for an acceptable sacrifice and then illogically applied them to human beings and our standards of beauty.

[2]Clinton E. Arnold, *ECNT: Ephesians* (Grand Rapids: Zondervan, 2010), 149.

[3]Noemi Vega Quiñones, *Hermanas: Deepening Our Identity and Growing Our Influence* (Downers Grove, IL: InterVarsity Press, 2019), 46, emphasis the author's.

[4]Vega Quiñones, *Hermanas*, 49.

[5]Natalia Kohn Rivera, *Hermanas*, 4.

[6]Kristy Garza Robinson, *Hermanas*, 6.

[7]Vega Quiñones, *Hermanas*, 6-7.

[8]Garza Robinson, *Hermanas*, 24.

[9]Michael Card, *Matthew: The Gospel of Identity* (Downers Grove, IL: Inter-Varsity Press, 2013), 20.

[10]Card, *Matthew*, 20.

[11]Card, *Matthew*, 21.

[12]Tisby, *The Color of Compromise*, 16.

[13]Christopher A. Porter, "2 Timothy," in *T&T Clark Social Identity Commentary on the New Testament*, eds. J. Brian Tucker and Aaron Kuecker (New York: T&T Clark, 2020), www.amazon.com/Clark-Social-Identity-Commentary -Testament/dp/0567667863.

[14]Neil Rendall, *Moses, God's Tri-Cultural Man*, InterVarsity Christian Fellowship /USA Multiethnic Ministries Bible study, accessed October 29, 2019, http:// mem.intervarsity.org/sites/mem/files/Moses%20-%20God%27s%20Tri -Cultural%20Man.pdf.

[15]Rendall, *Moses*, 4.

[16]Rendall, *Moses*, 5. These gifted folks would have included Moses' children by his Midianite wife, Zipporah. Their children would have been multiethnic and multicultural as well, and probably would have looked prototypically multi-ethnic. See Exodus 2, 4, and 18.

[17]Kathryn Lois Sullivan, as quoted by Elizabeth M. Davis, "Sullivan, Kathryn Lois (1905-2006)" in *Handbook of Women Biblical Interpreters: a Historical and Biographical Guide*, Marion Ann Taylor and Agnes Choi, eds. (Grand Rapids, MI: Baker Academic, 2012), 490.

6 EXPLORING AND NURTURING MIXED IDENTITY

[1]From InterVarsity Christian Fellowship/USA, "Process: Disciples Making Disciples," September 20, 2103, 2100.intervarsity.org/sites/2100/files/dis ciples%20make%20disciples_0.pdf.

[2]Ruth Haley Barton, *Invitation to Solitude and Silence: Experiencing God's Trans-forming Presence* (Downers Grove, IL: InterVarsity Press, 2004), 37-39.

[3]Jen has built on the work of Fuller Seminary Professor Daniel Lee, who com-bined *Poston's Biracial Identity Development Stages* and *Root's Resolutions for Resolving Otherness*.

[4]Leah Donnella, "A Festival For Mixed-Race Storytellers—And Everyone Else, Too," Code Switch, National Public Radio, June 20, 2016, www.npr.org /sections/codeswitch/2016/06/20/481373896/a-festival-for-mixed-race -storytellers-and-everyone-else-tooskdf.

[5]Stephanie Tait, quoting Nakita Valerio, Twitter post, March 30, 2019, 10:48 p.m., www.twitter.com/StephTaitWrites/status/1112200009989021702.

[6]See www.ignatianspirituality.com/ignatian-prayer/the-examen.

[7]Sally Lloyd-Jones, *The Jesus Storybook Bible* (Grand Rapids: Zondervan, 2007), 26.

7 MIXED IDENTITY IN OUR FAMILIES AND COMMUNITIES

[1]Grant Hilary Brenner, "Six Ways That a Rough Childhood Can Affect Adult Relationships," Psychology Today, July 1, 2017, www.psychologytoday.com/us /blog/experimentations/201707/6-ways-rough-childhood-can-affect -adult-relationships.

[2]Ellen Boeder, "Emotional Safety is Necessary for Emotional Connection," The Gottman Institute, August 4, 2017, www.gottman.com/blog/emotional-safety -is-necessary-for-emotional-connection/.

[3]Sundee Tucker Frazier, *Check All That Apply: Finding Wholeness as a Multiracial Person* (Downers Grove, IL: InterVarsity Press, 2002), Dedication.

[4]Cindy Wilson, *Too Much Soul: The Journey of an Asian Southern Belle* (Atlanta: Too Much Soul, 2018), 9.

[5]Wilson, *Too Much Soul*, 38.

[6]Wilson, *Too Much Soul*, 37.

[7]*National Geographic* also explored its own complicated history with race, which they addressed in the April 2018 issue, www.nationalgeographic.com /magazine/2018/04/from-the-editor-race-racism-history/. I think it's worth noting that they brought in an outside consultant to go over their archives, and that they clearly acknowledged their part in affirming White America in thinking that darker-skinned folks were "savages" and that Asian and Pacific Islanders—especially women—were exotic and alluring, among other harmful clichés. I mention this not by way of offering *National Geographic* an excuse for past racism, but once again in acknowledging that the crux of defeating racism lies in having a less polarized us/them mindset and more in the nonbinary worldview which mixed folks uniquely inhabit. As the editor's letter is titled: "For decades, our coverage was racist. To rise above our past, we must acknowledge it."

[8]*National Geographic*, "Black and White," www.nationalgeographic.com /magazine/2018/04/race-twins-black-white-biggs/.

[9]Daniel Lee, training session for InterVarsity Christian Fellowship, August 8, 2016, "The Asian American Quadrilateral."

[10]Jemar Tisby, *The Color of Compromise: The Truth about the American Church's Complicity in Racism* (Grand Rapids: Zondervan, 2019), 16-17, referencing Christena Cleveland, *Disunity in Christ: Uncovering the Hidden Forces That Keep Us Apart* (Downers Grove, IL: InterVarsity Press), 26-28.

[11]Frazier, *Check All That Apply*, 102.

[12]Robin DiAngelo, *White Fragility: Why It's So Hard for White People to Talk About Racism* (Boston: Beacon Press, 2018), 78-79. See also the Antiracism Research and Policy Center, founded by Ibram X. Kendi, at www .antiracismcenter.com.

8 MIXED IDENTITY IN THE CHURCH AND SOCIETY

[1]Christina Marie Quintanilla, "Prayer of a Mixed Woman," From the author's personal collection, 2017. Used with permission. All rights reserved.

[2]Jemar Tisby, *The Color of Compromise: The Truth About the American Church's Complicity in Racism* (Grand Rapids: Zondervan, 2019), 52.

[3]Richard Twiss, *One Church, Many Tribes: Following Jesus the Way God Made You* (Bloomington, MN: Chosen Books, 2015 edition), 125.

[4]Twiss, *One Church*, 125-26, emphasis mine.

[5]Even in 2019, some insurance and other official documents did not allow for checking multiple ethnicities.

[6]Daniel Hill, *White Awake: An Honest Look at What It Means to Be White* (Downers Grove, IL: InterVarsity Press, 2017), 4.

[7]Tisby, *The Color of Compromise*, 100.

[8]Brenda Salter McNeil, *Roadmap to Reconciliation: Moving Communities into Unity, Wholeness and Justice* (Downers Grove, IL: InterVarsity Press, 2015), 114.

[9]McNeil, *Roadmap to Reconciliation*, 114.

[10]Korie L. Edwards, *The Elusive Dream: The Power of Race in Interracial Churches* (New York: Oxford University Press, 2008), 56, 117-18.

[11]Efrem Smith, *The Post-Black and Post-White Church: Becoming the Beloved Community in a Multi-Ethnic World* (San Francisco: Jossey-Bass, 2012), electronic edition, 38-39.

[12]For example, the Nicene Creed or other classic Christian confessions of the faith.

[13]Z. E. Hawkinson, *Anatomy of the Pilgrim Experience: Reflections on Being a Covenanter* (Chicago: Covenant Publications, 2000), 14-15, as quoted by Smith in *The Post-Black*, electronic version, 125-26.

[14]"First parents" is a term used of biological parents to emphasize their dignity and importance in the lives of their children. I use the term "parents of color" to honor monoethnic, majority-culture parents who experience the unique intersectionality of raising children of color (through adoption, interracial marriage, or other means).

[15]Sandra Maria Van Opstal, *The Next Worship: Glorifying God in a Diverse World* (Downers Grove, IL: InterVarsity Press, 2016), 63.

[16]Soong-Chan Rah, *Prophetic Lament: A Call for Justice in Troubled Times* (Downers Grove, IL: InterVarsity Press, 2015), 22-24.

[17]Rah, *Prophetic Lament*, 209-10, emphasis mine.

[18]Van Opstal, *The Next Worship*, 141.

EPILOGUE: OUR STORY

[1]See the documentary *Between: Living in the Hyphen*, directed by Anne Marie Nakagawa (Montreal: National Film Board of Canada, 2005).

[2]"What Genetic Thread Do These Six Strangers Have in Common?," *National Geographic* video, March 18, 2018, youtu.be/csVywNHr7Vo.

[3]Poem written in conjunction with the "Where I'm From" Project, www.georgeellalyon.com/where.html.

Name Index

Italics indicate biblical figures

Subject Index

About the Author

Chandra Crane (BS Education, MA Ministry) is a multiethnic initiatives resource specialist with InterVarsity Christian Fellowship and a member of the multiethnic Redeemer Church in Jackson, Mississippi. Growing up in a multiethnic/multicultural family in the Southwest and now happily transplanted to the Deep South, Chandra is passionate about diversity and family.

She is in the Order of the Alumni with national forensics honorary fraternity Pi Kappa Delta and has achieved the Advanced Communicator Bronze award with Toastmasters International. She is a regular contributor for Dordt University's *In All Things* and has written for The Witness: A Black Christian Collective and InterVarsity's *The Well.* Chandra has spoken and led worship at several local and national InterVarsity conferences. She has also participated in online discussions for *Christianity Today.*

She is married to Kennan, a civil engineer, and they have two spunky daughters. Chandra is a fan of hot tea, crossword puzzles, Converse shoes, and science fiction. She thoroughly enjoys reading, napping, and defying stereotypes.

www.chandracrane.com
Twitter: @chandraLcrane
Instagram: @chandraLcrane and @MixedBlessingBook